ISBN: 978-0-9906957-0-7

SageWay Press
sagewaypress@gmail.com

Cover art: Andy Hoffman
Layout and design: lisadaly.com

How To Quote Shakespeare In Everyday Life

By Michael Denomme, Ph.D.

This book is dedicated to Lillian Denomme,
the warmest, sweetest mother a person
could ever hope to have. She is, quite simply,
the greatest person I have ever known.

ACKNOWLEDGEMENTS

Over the years a number of individuals have provided noteworthy support. Of the many friends who have been so helpful, I want to particularly acknowledge Joe Alff, Tom O'Hara and Dennis Roberts. These fellows had better things to do with their time than focus on my need for textual analysis, writing savvy, and sage advice; but they gave generously of their time anyway and with a kindness and warmth that make them the treasured friends they are. I am greatly indebted to Lisa Daly for her multi-talented book layout expertise and invaluable wise counsel. The book's engaging cover is the result of the superlative artistry of Andy Hoffman and the keen judgment of Bob Moore. I owe the back cover's photographs and whimsy to the ever-inventive Janice Moore. Over the years Doe Coover, Susan Magee, and Maryann Gorman provided important insight and perspective. When I finally arrived at a text, Alison DeLuca provided much-appreciated technical consultation.

Finally, as in so many ways throughout more than four decades of life partnership, the contributions of my wife, Sharon Denomme, have been indispensable. From painstakingly reading the manuscript, to patiently listening to my musings and concerns, to providing timely encouragement, she stepped forward with the same loving and thoughtful spirit that has always astounded me and enriched my life. To borrow from one of the many Shakespearean quotations featured in this book, on such connubial generosity "the gods themselves throw incense."

TABLE OF CONTENTS

CHAPTER 1. ROMANCE –
Heaven's Breath Smells Wooingly Here 5

    Totally Smitten. 5
    Contentment No Longer 6
    Resistance Is Futile. 8
    From Crass To Class 9
    The Audience Is Yours 10
    The Ways Of Seduction 12
    The Allure Is Everywhere 13
    Jealousy And Envy Rear Their Heads. 15
    Assorted Come-Ons And Wooing Techniques. . . . 16
    Hopelessly Devoted 18
    Love – Painful And Fleeting 19
    Crazy For Love. 21
    The Tempest Called Love 22

CHAPTER 2. COMPLIMENTS AND INSULTS –
The Mirror Of All Courtesy – And Not 25

    ### CLASSY COMPLIMENTS 25
    Candid Beauty 25
    Absolutely Gorgeous. 27
    The Eye Of Beauty 29
    Beyond Good-Looking 31
    A Beautiful Complexion 32
    Beauty – Full Of Grace. 33
    Setting The Style. 35

In Praise Of Leadership 36

Cool And Deliberate 38

Elegant Insults 39

Beauty's Decline 39

Beauty's Deceit 40

The Obnoxious Male 42

The Superficial 43

The Untrustworthy 44

The Foolish 45

The Puffed-Up 46

The Long-Winded 48

The Sharp-Tongued 49

Not So Elegant Insults 50

An Array Of Faults 50

A Pathetic Display 51

Chapter 3. Marriage, Family And Friends –
Not Another Comfort Like To This 55

Marriage 55

Taking The Plunge 55

Connubial Bliss 57

A Gem Of A Spouse 58

Expectations And The Lowering Thereof 59

Yes, Dear 61

Marital Cynics 62

Family 63

Parental Exasperation 64

Tough Love 65

The Scheming Never Ends 66
Kids Will Be Kids 68

FRIENDS 69
A Special Joy 69

CHAPTER 4. THE WORK-A-DAY WORLD –
So Foul And Fair A Day 73
Wise Office Strategies 73
Wily Office Strategies 75
Co-Worker Flaws. 76
Comeuppance Time 77
Workday Anxiety. 79
Deception All Around 80
Praising Exceptional Work. 82
Embracing Contradictions 83
Mentoring With Care 84

CHAPTER 5. RECREATION AND TRAVEL –
The Pert And Nimble Spirit 87
RECREATION 87
Entering The Fray 87
When The Battle Is Over 89
To Have What It Takes 91
Focusing Your Energy 92

TRAVEL 93
Kicking Back And Relaxing 94
Diving Into Pleasure 95
Enjoying Nature 97

CHAPTER 6. DAILY THEATRICS –
All The World's A Stage

CHAPTER 6. DAILY THEATRICS –
All The World's A Stage 99

Bemoaning One's Fate 99
Bemoaning A Mutual Fate 102
Risk Taking 104
Preparing To Trounce The Opposition 105
Sucking It Up 106
Going Into Battle 107
Displaying Courage .108
Exchanging Barbs 110
Stepping Up To The Plate 111
Hamming It Up 112
Really Hamming It Up 113
Rising To The Pomposity Occasion 114
Reckoning With Fortune 116
Putting Reputation On Trial 117
Staying Above The Crowd 119
Maneuvering Deviously 120

CHAPTER 7. SERIOUSLY NOW –
The Abundant Dolor Of The Heart 123

A Brief And Elegant Eulogy 123
In Touch With Grief 125
Unspeakable Anguish 126
Expressing Sorrow .128
Coping With Life's Trials 129
Willing To Pay The Price 131
A Beautiful Goodbye 132

CHAPTER 8. WISE COUNSEL -
We'll Teach You To Drink Deep 135

    In Times Of Adversity 135

    All In Due Time 137

    Heavenly Intervention 138

    Probing Life's Mysteries 140

    Everything In Moderation 142

    Whatever Will Be, Will Be 143

    Hanging Tough 144

    Human Frailty 145

    The Value Of Suffering 147

    Expectations Turned Upside Down 148

    Patience Is A Virtue 149

    Sage Advice 151

    Show Me The Money 152

CHAPTER 9. FIFTY WAYS TO LOVE YOUR SHAKESPEARE

    1. Playing The Wise Philosopher 155

    2. Mocking The Blowhard 156

    3. Scorning The Bore 156

    4. Insulting The Windbag 157

    5. Disdaining The Pampered 157

    6. Listening Attentively 158

    7. Giving Romance Its Due 158

    8. Resisting Temptation 159

    9. Sounding The Scoundrel Alarm 160

   10. Inviting Intimacy 160

   11. Embracing Ecstasy 161

12. Denouncing A Cad 161
13. Walking On Air 162
14. Making Up Passionately. 163
15. Hiding The Truth 163
16. Engaging The Romantic Battle 164
17. Dispensing Praise 165
18. Delivering A Classy Send-Off. 165
19. Decrying Indifference. 166
20. Reaffirming Your Affection. 166
21. Challenging A Foe. 167
22. Arriving At Wisdom. 167
23. Gushing With Enthusiasm 168
24. Celebrating Courage 169
25. Meeting Calamity Head-On 169
26. Promoting Leisure. 170
27. Criticizing A Nasty Tongue. 170
28. Chiding Inconsiderate Offspring 171
29. Faking Contentment 172
30. Staying Above It All 172
31. Being True To Yourself 173

32. Going With Your Gut 174

33. Challenging Narrow Thinking 174

34. Bursting An Overconfident Bubble. 175

35. Rationalizing Bad Behavior 176

36. Finishing What You've Started 176

37. Showing Good Judgment 177

38. Putting Yourself In God's Hands 178

39. Loving In A Balanced Way 178

40. Confronting Terror 179

41. Discovering Your Own Pain 179

42. Skewering Expertise. 180

43. Grumbling About Your Job 180

44. Seeking Liquid Solace 181

45. Grieving A Loss 181

46. Focusing On What You Love 182

47. Taking The Mature Approach 183

48. Letting Others Shine 184

49. Making Blissful Love Again. 184

50. Finding The Sweetness 185

INDEX TO KEY WORDS AND PHRASES 187

INTRODUCTION

Wouldn't you love to make vivid descriptions and sparkling repartee your trademark? Wouldn't it be sweet, time and again, to come up with a great turn of phrase at just the right moment? Of course it would. But sadly, all too often, what you actually find yourself doing is using the same trite expressions that everyone else employs. You'd love your conversation to be more inventive and resourceful, but where can you turn to get the edge you need? The answer comes from our most revered writer, although one whose language is typically seen as too lofty or too old-fashioned for modern usage – none other than the Elizabethan master himself, William Shakespeare.

The value of Shakespeare as cultural enjoyment has long been established. His plays are continually produced throughout the world, and the cinema has long embraced him as one of its favorites. In the hands of English director Kenneth Branagh, for example, the plays *Henry V, Much Ado About Nothing, Hamlet, Love's Labour's Lost,* and *As You Like It* have been brought to the screen with a deft touch and often surprising commercial success. *Shakespeare in Love,* the imagined story of the Bard's great love, won an Academy Award for best picture. And Shakespearean plots in modern dress, like *10 Things I Hate About You* and *She's the Man,* have found an eager audience. Even the world of animation has gotten into the act with *Gnomeo and Juliet.* Still, it's one thing to enjoy entertainment by or about Shakespeare. It's quite another to use his words in everyday conversation. After all, he did write over four hundred years ago. Is it really true, you say to yourself, that Shakespeare can be of genuinely practical use to me in my daily life? Aren't you glad the answer is a resounding YES?

The purpose of this book is to demonstrate in a very practical way that Shakespeare, with his richness of imagery and depth of psychological insight, is remarkably adaptable to modern times. It's true that we will be taking some liberties with the Shakespearean texts. We may take some words or phrases intentionally out of context. We may even take an image or concept and intentionally ascribe a different meaning than our Elizabethan ancestors would recognize. And, yes, we'll change a word here or drop a phrase there. But it will all be in the service of a worthy goal: to enrich the playful, poignant and sublime moments of our lives with Shakespeare's marvelous array of words and images.

It is important to realize, however, that the Elizabethan world in which Shakespeare lived had dramatically different views on a number of issues of fundamental importance to modern society. For example, although many of Shakespeare's greatest characters were women, the English environment in which he lived was far removed from modern sensibilities with respect to their role and status. And certainly, while Elizabethan society was much bawdier than our common perceptions of it, the environment was quite different from our own with respect to sexuality in general. So, in an effort to reflect a contemporary approach to these matters, I have found it necessary to do some "stretching" when it comes to using Shakespeare's words to address these issues. Purists may recoil in horror; but, of course, they will have already recoiled from many other perceived sacrileges.

To achieve our goal, this book features nearly 150 scenarios that depict modern life, from working for an odious boss to vacationing in an island paradise, from romancing till dawn to picking up after the kids. They're all here – the pleasures, the headaches, the heartaches, and the humor of living in today's world. Each of these scenarios is preceded by at least one commonplace expression, idiom or cliché that would typically be used in facing the situation. A quotation from Shakespeare then follows. These quotes from the Bard are not intended to be exact equivalents in meaning to the conventional expressions, although they may be astonishing close; instead they represent an alternate way of addressing the scenario. Since the lead person in the scenario may be either male or female, you will need to make the gender adjustment that best works for you. Because individuals of differing ages, genders, sexual orientations, and economic circumstances will be reading these scenarios, I have intentionally switched scenario protagonists throughout the book. My hope is that each reader, from time to time, may be able to place himself or herself directly in the scenario. Of course, this also means that the ubiquitous "you" of a given scenario may or may not be directly applicable to each reader's life situation. In my view this only adds to the fun because we all get to tune into how a wide range of people can effectively employ Shakespeare's words in their daily lives. It does require all of us to be quite imaginative, but then who else would have the slightest interest in quoting Shakespeare in everyday life in the first place?

Following most scenarios are couplets that consist of common everyday expressions with their Shakespearean alternatives – over 300 in all. These couplets await the opportunity to star in their own scenarios as you reflect on the specific situations and circumstances of your daily life.

As you learn how to use Shakespeare to illuminate and enrich your own life events, you will find yourself responding in a much more interesting, amusing or creative way to a wide range of life circumstances. You'll stop putting Shakespeare on a pedestal and put him where he belongs – on the tip of your tongue.

How To Quote Shakespeare In Everyday Life is not an academic exercise – it is a practical, useable guide to employing Shakespeare's extraordinary imagery to transform the commonplace speech of your daily life. You can make vivid descriptions and sparkling repartee your trademark.

A Note About The Shakespearean Text

I have chosen *The Riverside Shakespeare, 2nd Edition*, as the Shakespearean text. I wanted a single-volume edition of the complete works that is readily available, and the Riverside is the finest one I know. It is beautifully researched with terrific explanatory footnotes for anyone who wants to delve a little more deeply into Shakespeare's words and imagery. But the price I've paid for this choice is that we will be using a text that is based on a scrupulous adherence to the original Shakespearean word construction. The result is a certain number of archaic spellings and contractions. These strange Elizabethan forms may well be confusing at times to you and to the recipients of your newly inspired word play. So I've decided to modernize, without comment, a relatively small number of words and punctuation marks that might prove too perplexing, annoying, or obscure. Not a big deal for most of us perhaps. But to Shakespearean dogmatists such irreverence may not go down smoothly. Too bad for them. They are about to miss out on a whole lot of fun.

Chapter 1. Romance –
Heaven's Breath Smells Wooingly Here

Ah, the exhilarating madness of falling in love. No words can truly capture its allure, but do you really have to settle for one cliché after another in trying to describe it? Of course you don't. These are the grand moments of passion. Prepare to serve them up with the special verbal seasoning that is the Bard's trademark.

Totally Smitten

GOODBYE TRITENESS:
Now I know what true love is.

HELLO INSPIRATION:
Did my heart love till now? Forswear it, sight!
For I never saw true beauty till this night.
~ *Romeo and Juliet* (I.v.52-53).

You've just been on a date with the person of your dreams, and you both had a fantastic time. Your best friend, knowing your tendency to get carried away in matters of the heart, suggests you play it cool. But you're not buying it. Disdaining caution, on the very next morning, you send an e-mail with the above quote as its ardent centerpiece. Then you smoothly add: "We sure had a great time last night. Let's keep the magic going this weekend."

Other Couplets – *For The Helplessly In Love*

COMMON:

If it's really love, you'll know it immediately.

TRANSFORMED:

Who ever loved that loved not at first sight?

~ *As You Like It* (III.v.82).

COMMON:

She/he's my whole world.

TRANSFORMED:

My food, my fortune, and my sweet hope's aim.

~ *The Comedy of Errors* (III.ii.63).

COMMON:

I'm obsessed with him.

TRANSFORMED:

O, know'st thou not his looks are my soul's food?

~ *The Two Gentlemen of Verona* (II.vii.15).

Contentment No Longer

NOT THE OBVIOUS:

I just can't stop thinking about her/him.

BUT THE EXCEPTIONAL:

O now, forever
Farewell the tranquil mind! farewell content!

~ *Othello* (III.iii.347-348).

The smoke from your earlobes has yet to recede, and your constant smiling has managed to annoy even your best friends. So, after another fabulously romantic weekend, wait no longer to send an e-mail or card to your marvelous lover featuring the above quote. Feel free to conclude with these words: "Contentment's a bore. I'd rather be driven crazy thinking about you."

OTHER COUPLETS – *No Peace To Be Found*

COMMON:

When I was young, I suffered a lot of heartache.

TRANSFORMED:

Truly in my youth I suffered much extremity for love.

~ *Hamlet* (II.ii.189-190).

COMMON:

In your youth, you pined away for love.

TRANSFORMED:

In thy youth thou wast as true a lover
As ever sighed upon a midnight pillow.

~ *As You Like It* (II.iv.26-27).

COMMON:

The pleasure is not worth the price.

TRANSFORMED:

One fading moment's mirth
With twenty watchful, weary, tedious nights.

~ *The Two Gentlemen of Verona* (I.i.29-31).

COMMON:

You'll never be at peace again.

TRANSFORMED:

Not… all the drowsy syrups of the world
Shall ever medicine thee to that sweet sleep
Which thou owned yesterday.

~ *Othello* (III.iii.330-333).

Resistance Is Futile

REJECT THE MUNDANE:

One look from you and I'm undone.

AND EMBRACE THE ENCHANTING:

Alack, there lies more peril in thine eye
Than twenty of their swords!

~ *Romeo and Juliet* (II.ii.71-72).

A pleasant night of trashing faithless lovers is brought to a halt when an old flame, still smolderingly hot, saunters into Chumley's Bar. After your latest romantic fiasco, the last thing you need is yet another plunge into those precarious waters. So, naturally, after carefully considering all of your options, you throw caution to the wind and start heading in the direction of ecstasy and doom. Your friends, knowing what jeopardy lurks, try to stop you. You respond: "I know there lies more peril in those eyes than all other dangers combined. But I simply have no power to resist."

OTHER COUPLETS – *There's No Escape*

COMMON:
>*She has become an absolute addiction.*

TRANSFORMED:
>**Age cannot wither her, nor custom stale**
>**Her infinite variety. Other women cloy**
>**The appetites they feed, but she makes hungry**
>**Where most she satisfies.**
>~ *Antony and Cleopatra* (II.ii.234-237).

COMMON:
>*He's her boy toy.*

TRANSFORMED:
>**[He] is become the bellows and the fan**
>**To cool a gypsy's lust.**
>~ *Antony and Cleopatra* (I.i.9-10).

COMMON:
>*I fell head over heels in love.*

TRANSFORMED:
>**My woman's heart**
>**Grossly grew captive to his honey words.**
>~ *Richard III* (IV.i.78-79).

From Crass To Class

SPARE US THE BOORISH:
>*Hot to trot.*

AND SHOW SOME ELEGANCE:
>**A votary to fond desire.**
>~ *The Two Gentlemen of Verona* (I.i.52).

Others may display their crudity by referring to how "horny" they are. Instead you suggest that you are a person fervently devoted to love: "a votary to fond desire." Same hormones, better style.

Other Couplets – *Tastefully Done*

COMMON:
Doing the mattress mambo.

TRANSFORMED:
... Honeying and making love.
~ *Hamlet* (III.iv.93).

COMMON:
Get some sugar.

TRANSFORMED:
Steal immortal blessing from her lips.
~ *Romeo and Juliet* (III.iii.37).

The Audience Is Yours

PROCLAIM UNCONVINCINGLY:
This relationship is exhausting.

OR SHAMELESSLY INDULGE:
Under love's heavy burden do I sink.
~ *Romeo and Juliet* (I.iv.22).

You and your girlfriends are at the Bistro de Parfait for a drink when your fiancé calls with a request that you join him for another business dinner, this time at the most expensive restaurant in town.

Although you thoroughly enjoy such dinners, you can't resist playing the victim to the hilt: "Once again, I've got to get dressed up and go out to another fancy restaurant tonight. Truly the Bard was right – 'under love's heavy burden do I sink.'" Your amusing deception is sure to be duly noted by your drinking companions. As they prepare to give you what you so richly deserve, you may choose to make a well-advised and immediate beeline for the door.

OTHER COUPLETS – *A Bit Over The Top*

COMMON:

I just can't bear this much happiness.

TRANSFORMED:

O love, be moderate, allay thy ecstasy,
In measure rein thy joy, scant this excess!
I feel too much thy blessing; make it less,
For fear I surfeit.

~ *The Merchant of Venice* (III.ii.111-114).

COMMON:

I'll never stop loving you.

TRANSFORMED:

Doubt thou the stars are fire,
Doubt that the sun doth move,
Doubt truth to be a liar,
But never doubt I love.

~ *Hamlet* (II.ii.116-119).

The Ways Of Seduction

SPARE US THE COARSE:

She's coming on to me.

AND GIVE US THE REFINED:

Her eye discourses, I will answer it.

~ *Romeo and Juliet* (II.ii.13).

Your lack of romantic adventures has plunged you into the dumps again. So it's off to Scoobies Bar where you are determined to surrender yourself to the solace of the grape. Then, it happens – a highly attractive woman walks by your table and, you insist, gives you a "come hither" look you simply can't ignore. You turn to your faithful (soon to be dumfounded) friends and say, "Her eye discourses; I will answer it." Lesser mortals might then proceed to make total fools of themselves; but you, in your new role as Shakespearean smoothie, are certain to escape this fate. Yes, sir, no doubt about it.

OTHER COUPLETS – *Making One's Move*

COMMON:

He's constantly saying how much he loves me.

TRANSFORMED:

He hath of late made many tenders
Of his affection to me.

~ *Hamlet* (I.iii.99-100).

COMMON:

Out on the town, looking for some action.

TRANSFORMED:

In the lusty stealth of nature.

~ *King Lear* (I.ii.11).

The Allure Is Everywhere

TEDIOUSLY SIGH:

It seems like I'm always falling in love.

OR CLEVERLY ASSERT:

Full many a lady
I have eyed with best regard, and many a time
The harmony of their tongues hath into bondage
Brought my too diligent ear.

~ *The Tempest* (III.i.39-42).

Things are going quite well, thank you, in the romance department these days. So naturally you are, in mock seriousness, bemoaning your fate to a friend. The full quote, as is, may suit you perfectly; but you could choose to make the following adjustment: "Full many a lady/gentleman have I eyed with best regard, and many a time the harmony of their forms has brought into bondage my too diligent eye." Oh, the agony!

Other Couplets – *Refrain Or Not?*

COMMON:

I'd love to get her in the sack!

TRANSFORMED:

Now, by the world, it is a lusty wench!...
O, how I long to have some chat with her!
~ *The Taming of the Shrew* (II.i.160-162).

COMMON:

We need to get our passions under control.

TRANSFORMED:

We have... to cool our raging motions,
our carnal stings, our unbitted lusts.
~ *Othello* (I.iii.335).

COMMON:

He's only interested in her body.

TRANSFORMED:

Young men's love then lies
Not truly in their hearts, but in their eyes.
~ *Romeo and Juliet* (II.iii.67-68).

COMMON:

Everything is about sex.

TRANSFORMED:

It is a bawdy planet.
~ *The Winter's Tale* (I.ii.201).

Jealousy And Envy Rear Their Heads

ANYONE CAN SAY:

You're being eaten up with jealousy.

THAT'S WHY YOU SAY:

O, beware ... of jealousy!
It is the green-eyed monster, which doth mock
The meat it feeds on.

~ *Othello* (III.iii.165-167).

Your friend's jealousy regarding his or her lover is completely unfounded. Your status as best friend and chief buttinsky requires that you try to bring some sanity to the situation. Shakespeare will give you your opening lines, but don't expect this medicine to go down smoothly.

OTHER COUPLETS – *When Love Turns Green*

COMMON:

He/she loved to excess.

TRANSFORMED:

One that loved not wisely but too well.

~ *Othello* (V.ii.344).

COMMON:

The jealous will believe anything.

TRANSFORMED:

Trifles light as air
Are to the jealous confirmations strong
As proofs of holy writ.

~ *Othello* (III.iii.322-24).

COMMON:

Jealousy will ruin everything.

TRANSFORMED:

This canker that eats up Love's tender spring.

~ *Venus and Adonis* (656).

COMMON:

It's killing me to see him/her so happy!

TRANSFORMED:

O, how bitter a thing it is to look into happiness through another man's eyes!

~ *As You Like It* (V.ii.43-45).

Assorted Come-Ons And Wooing Techniques

WE'VE ALL HEARD THIS BEFORE:

Let's do it – we're only young once.

BUT NOT THIS:

What is love? 'Tis not hereafter;
Present mirth hath present laughter;
What's to come is still unsure:
In delay there lies no plenty,
Then come kiss me, sweet and twenty
Youth's a stuff will not endure.

~ *Twelfth Night* (II.iii.47-52).

The perfect six liner for the man or woman who would like to urge a companion toward greater intimacy. Since the object of affection is unlikely to be the exact age described in the poem, you may want to change "sweet and twenty" to "ardently."

OTHER COUPLETS – *You've Got To Have The Right Style*

COMMON:

You sure look great today.

TRANSFORMED:

Shall I compare thee to a summer's day?
Thou art more lovely and more temperate.

~ *Sonnet 18* (1-2).

COMMON:

Let me speak clearly: I love you.

TRANSFORMED:

I know no ways to mince it in love,
but directly to say, "I love you."

~ *Henry V* (V.ii.126-127).

COMMON:

Let's have some music.

TRANSFORMED:

If music be the food of love, play on.

~ *Twelfth Night* (I.i.1).

and

Give me some music; music, moody food
Of us that trade in love.

~ *Antony and Cleopatra* (II.v.1-2).

COMMON:

What a delightful fragrance.

TRANSFORMED:

Heaven's breath
Smells wooingly here.

~ *Macbeth* (I.vi.5-6).

Hopelessly Devoted

INCREDULOUSLY ASK:

So you can easily resist temptation, eh?

OR BOLDLY QUESTION:

Is this the nature
Whom passion could not shake?

~ *Othello* (IV.i.265-266).

Your friend, well known for his or her expressed intention not to surrender to the enticements of romance, has fallen hopelessly in love. After hearing the tale of infatuation, you cannot resist a gently teasing rendition of "Is this the nature whom passion could not shake?" Then, lest you be accounted a boor, you quickly follow it up with hearty congratulations. Save the snickering for later.

OTHER COUPLETS – *Head Over Heels*

COMMON:

He's wild about her.

TRANSFORMED:

He hath devoted and given up himself to the
contemplation, mark, and denotement of
her parts and graces.

~ *Othello* (II.iii.316-318).

COMMON:

He's making an ass of himself for her.

TRANSFORMED:

**Take but good note, and you shall see in him [a] …
pillar of the world transformed
Into a strumpet's fool.**

~ *Antony and Cleopatra* (I.i.11-13).

COMMON:

She/he has got it real bad.

TRANSFORMED:

In love, in faith, to the very tip of the nose.

~ *Troilus and Cressida* (III.i.127).

COMMON:

Your love is everything to me.

TRANSFORMED:

The crown and comfort of my life, your favor.

~ *The Winter's Tale* (III.ii.94).

Love – Painful And Fleeting

STOP WHINING:

Just wait until someone breaks your heart.

AND WISELY COMMENT:

**Then shall you know the wounds invisible
That love's keen arrows make.**

~ *As You Like It* (III.v.30-31).

Enduring the romantic heave-ho is bad enough without insensitive fools showing no sympathy for your travail. You're tired of being the object of derision, so you go on the offensive with a righteous lecture on "the wounds invisible that love's keen arrows make." Of course, they may now hate you for showing them up with Shakespeare; but wouldn't you rather be despised than pitied?

OTHER COUPLETS – *Heartbreaking And Brief*

COMMON:

Let's go and cry our eyes out.

TRANSFORMED:

**Let us seek out some desolate shade, and there
Weep our sad bosoms empty.**

~ *Macbeth* (IV.iii.1-2).

COMMON:

Passion doesn't last forever.

TRANSFORMED:

**There lives within the very flame of love
A kind of wick or snuff that will abate it.**

~ *Hamlet* (IV.vii.114-115).

COMMON:

She'll tire of him sooner or later.

TRANSFORMED:

**When she is sated with his body, she will
find the error of her choice.**

~ *Othello* (I.iii.350-351).

Crazy For Love

SPARE US:
The helpless victim of her charms.

AND INTRIGUE WITH:
The noble ruin of her magic.
~ Antony and Cleopatra (III.x.18).

Old Harry just has not been the same. Formerly the most free-spirited of fellows who always had time for a night out with the boys at the Easy Elbow Tavern, he now seems to be completely under the well-manicured thumb of the fabulous Sheila. "Poor Harry," says your sympathetic friend Wilbur, "Sheila's got him so under her spell he doesn't know whether he's coming or going. I really feel sorry for him." "Yes, indeed," you respond, "behold Harry, 'the noble ruin of her magic'." Now, if only "poor" Harry would just stop smiling.

OTHER COUPLETS – *It's Just Insane*

COMMON:
Love makes you go nuts.

TRANSFORMED:
Love is merely a madness, and I tell you, deserves as well a dark house and a whip as madmen do.
~ As You Like It (III.ii.400-402).

COMMON:
When we're in love, we sure do wacky things sometimes.

TRANSFORMED:
We that are true lovers run into strange capers.
~ As You Like It (II.iv.54-55).

COMMON:

They're all the same – out of their minds!

TRANSFORMED:

The lunatic, the lover, and the poet
Are of imagination all compact.

~ A Midsummer Night's Dream (V.i.7-8).

COMMON:

He/she will say anything in the heat of passion.

TRANSFORMED:

When the blood burns, how prodigal the soul
lends the tongue vows.

~ Hamlet (I.iii.116-117).

The Tempest Called Love

DISPENSE A PLATITUDE:

They're playing with dynamite.

OR ASTONISH WITH YOUR ERUDITION:

These violent delights have violent ends,
And in their triumph die, like fire and powder,
Which as they kiss consume.

~ Romeo and Juliet (II.vi.9-11).

You know a spirited couple that loves to live life in the fast lane. Theirs is a tempestuous relationship where both the fires of passion and the fires of anger burn equally bright. Now, they've just had a real doozy of a fight, and this time it looks like it's truly over. Your comment is the above quote with perhaps the addition of these words: "No one could sustain that intensity. They were bound to consume each other."

OTHER COUPLETS – *It's Never Dull*

COMMON:

Our relationship is quite a roller coaster.

TRANSFORMED:

Thou and I are too wise to woo peaceably.

~ *Much Ado About Nothing* (V.ii.72).

COMMON:

Love has its ups and downs.

TRANSFORMED:

The course of true love never did run smooth.

~ *A Midsummer Night's Dream* (I.i.134).

CHAPTER 2.
COMPLIMENTS AND INSULTS –
The Mirror Of All Courtesy – And Not

You are about to astonish family, friends and co-workers with one display after another of pure Shakespearean incandescence. It goes without saying that, after a few of these perfect little gems, they'll be begging for more.

CLASSY COMPLIMENTS
Candid Beauty

SOUND LIKE A CONCEITED ASS:
I've got a great body.

OR SAY IT WITH TRUE PANACHE:
'Tis known I am a pretty piece of flesh.
~ *Romeo and Juliet* (I.i.29).

For a number of months now, you have been dieting and vigorously working out at the gym – all to get ready for your ten-year class reunion. At your last reunion you were not, if truth be told, in peak form. But now you're looking fabulous in a spectacular dress and are ready to strut your stuff. At the party, smarmy Alice sidles over and, with distinct lack of class, expresses surprise at how great you look. You can't resist retorting with the toothiest smile you can muster, "Well 'tis known I am a pretty piece of flesh." Feel free to conclude with "Eat your heart out."

OTHER COUPLETS –
Because "Hunk" And "Babe" Don't Cut It

COMMON:

Quite attractive.

TRANSFORMED:

Framed as fruitful as the free elements.

~ *Othello* (II.iii.341-342).

COMMON:

Well-built.

TRANSFORMED:

Framed in the prodigality of nature.

~ *Richard III* (I.ii.243).

COMMON:

What a voluptuous figure.

TRANSFORMED:

So divine, so full replete with choice of all delights.

~ *Henry VI, Part One* (V.v.16-17).

COMMON:

Very shapely.

TRANSFORMED:

**Her fine foot, straight leg, and quivering thigh,
And the demesnes that there adjacent lie.**

~ *Romeo and Juliet* (II.i.19-20).

[Note: "Demesnes" should be modernized to "domains."]

Absolutely Gorgeous

TRUE, BUT JOIN THE THRONG:

What a beauty.

OR SEPARATE YOURSELF FROM THE CROWD:

Most radiant, exquisite, and unmatchable beauty.

~ *Twelfth Night* (I.v.170-171).

and

**Thou hast a lady far more beautiful
Than any woman in this waning age.**

~ *The Taming of the Shrew* (Induction.ii.62-63).

and

For her own person, it beggared all description.

~ *Antony and Cleopatra* (II.ii.197-198).

These quotes manage to be simple and yet elegant at the same time. They are great for a quick compliment, a brief note or e-mail, or a special event card. For example, you could combine two of the quotes this way: "As the Bard has said, she is 'a lady far more beautiful than any woman in this waning age,' truly a woman of 'radiant, exquisite and unmatchable beauty.'" If you feel you just can't find the words to describe how beautiful or remarkable a person is, just say that her or his amazing qualities "beggar all description."

OTHER COUPLETS – *Imagery To Match The Grandeur*

COMMON:

A woman who is positively dazzling.

TRANSFORMED:

A maid
That paragons description and wild fame.
~ *Othello* (II.i.61-62).

COMMON:

The essence of splendor.

TRANSFORMED:

The heart-blood of beauty, love's invisible soul.
~ *Troilus and Cressida* (III.i.32-33).

COMMON:

She has no equal anywhere.

TRANSFORMED:

Her whom we know well
The world's large spaces cannot parallel.
~ *Troilus and Cressida* (II.ii.161-162).

COMMON:

The springtime of her fascination.

TRANSFORMED:

The lovely April of her prime.

~ *Sonnet 3* (10).

COMMON:

Sheer enchantment.

TRANSFORMED:

The holiday-time of [her] beauty.

~ *The Merry Wives of Windsor* (II.i.2).

COMMON:

No one could be more lovely.

TRANSFORMED:

One fairer than my love! The all-seeing sun
Never saw her match since first the world begun.

~ *Romeo and Juliet* (I.ii.92-93).

The Eye Of Beauty

TOO STALE:

Women's eyes are so captivating.

SUPERBLY FRESH:

From women's eyes this doctrine I derive:
… They are the books, the arts, the academes,
That show, contain, and nourish all the world.

~ *Love's Labor's Lost* (IV.iii.347-350).

You've been working on a very difficult and time-consuming project the entire week and have thoroughly neglected the love of your life in the process. It's time to make amends big time. First, you send an e-mail to your sweetheart announcing a discovery that makes all of your former work pale in insignificance. You promise that details will soon follow. Then, after a short pause, you send a second e-mail that includes the above quote, taking pains to change "from women's eyes" to the name of your beloved. She may laugh at this comparison of her eyes to the font of all knowledge, truth and wisdom; but, unless you are really in the doghouse, you will have secured her attention. The next move is up to you.

OTHER COUPLETS – *A Vision That Is Pure Poetry*

COMMON:

Bright-eyed as the sun.

TRANSFORMED:

Her eyes in heaven
Would through the airy region stream so bright
That birds would sing and think it were not night.

~ *Romeo and Juliet* (II.ii.20-22).

COMMON:

The seductive magic of your eyes.

TRANSFORMED:

The heavenly rhetoric of thine eye.

~ *Love's Labor's Lost* (IV.iii.58).

COMMON:

Eyes that speak volumes of love.

TRANSFORMED:

Your eyes, where I o'erlook
Love's stories written in Love's richest book.

~ *A Midsummer Night's Dream* (II.ii.121-122).

Beyond Good-Looking

ENSURE BANALITY:

He is handsome inside and out.

OR CHOOSE TO FASCINATE:

I do not think
So fair an outward and such stuff within
Endows a man but he.

~ *Cymbeline* (I.i.22-23).

Your best friend's new boyfriend is quite the handsome fellow. And, furthermore, as she never tires of pointing out, he also seems to be quite thoughtful and kind. Not currently in a relationship yourself, you could choose to go down the path of petty envy. It's touch and go, but you resist. Instead you decide to employ the above quote in your own gracious assessment of his qualities. Sweetly done, indeed!

OTHER COUPLETS – *Beyond Skin Deep*

COMMON:

I pale in comparison to him.

TRANSFORMED:

He hath a daily beauty in his life
That makes me ugly.

~ *Othello* (V.i.19-20).

COMMON:

In the end, it's character that matters.

TRANSFORMED:

A good leg will fall, a straight back will stoop... a fair face will wither... but a good heart... is the sun and the moon.

~ *Henry V* (V.ii.159-163).

COMMON:

Handsome is as handsome does.

TRANSFORMED:

In nature there's no blemish but the mind; none can be called deformed but the unkind.

~ *Twelfth Night* (III.iv.367-368).

A Beautiful Complexion

ANY CLOD COULD SAY TO HER:

You still look great.

INSTEAD YOU TURN HER HEAD WITH:

Beauty's ensign yet
Is crimson in thy lips and in thy cheeks.

~ *Romeo and Juliet* (V.iii.94-95).

Your lady, always radiantly beautiful to you, is seated in front of the mirror, sadly surveying the results of an exhausting week at work. Eager to lift her spirits, you walk over and put a hand on her shoulder. You then proceed to perform some poetic surgery on her broken self-image with "beauty's ensign yet is crimson in your lips and in your cheeks." Beautiful. No need to mention that when Romeo uttered these words he thought (falsely) that his beloved Juliet was, how shall we say, quite dead!

OTHER COUPLETS – *Such Lovely Skin*

COMMON:

What wonderful coloring.

TRANSFORMED:

'Tis beauty truly blent, whose red and white
Nature's own sweet and cunning hand laid on.
~ *Twelfth Night* (I.v.239-240).

COMMON:

Her skin is glowing.

TRANSFORMED:

The brightness of her cheek would shame those stars
As daylight doth a lamp.
~ *Romeo and Juliet* (II.ii.19-20).

Beauty – Full Of Grace

GRACELESSLY SUBDUED:

Quite taken with her personality.

GRACIOUSLY ADEPT:

In her strong toil of grace.
~ *Antony and Cleopatra* (V.ii.348).

Your buddy Bill has been going out with a lovely woman who has captivated him so completely that he wants to spend virtually all of his time with her. Somehow he no longer finds the time for endless rounds of burgers, beers, and football with you and the guys. You are envious of his good fortune and, consequently, can't wait to say something snide about it. So, when he is within earshot, you "whisper" to the fellows that it's such a shame that he is caught in Tina's "strong toil of grace" and can't act for himself. The fact that you'd suck a bowling ball through a straw for a chance to change places with dear William need not be discussed at this time.

OTHER COUPLETS – *The Graceful Words You Need*

COMMON:

She takes my breath away.

TRANSFORMED:

[She is] possessed with such a gentle sovereign grace,
Of such enchanting presence and discourse.
~ *The Comedy of Errors* (III.ii.160-161).

COMMON:

One classy lady.

TRANSFORMED:

A maid of grace and complete majesty.
~ *Love's Labor's Lost* (I.i.137).

COMMON:

What a marvelous woman.

TRANSFORMED:

Bethink thee on her virtues that surmount,
[And] natural graces that extinguish art.
~ *Henry VI, Part One* (V.iii.191-192).

COMMON:

Such an exquisite face.

TRANSFORMED:

See what a grace was seated on this brow.
~ *Hamlet* (III.iv.55).

COMMON:

An elegant air.

TRANSFORMED:

The cool and temperate wind of grace.

~ *Henry V* (III.iii.30).

COMMON:

Developed into an incredible person.

TRANSFORMED:

Now grown in grace
Equal with wondering.

~ *The Winter's Tale* (IV.i.24-25).

Setting The Style

UNIMAGINATIVE:

He/she is the fashion plate of the group.

STRIKING:

He was indeed the glass
Wherein the noble youth did dress themselves.

~ *Henry IV, Part Two* (II.iii.21-22).

It's your class reunion, and you have just spotted the woman whose sense of style and sophistication as a teenager was the envy of all the other girls in high school. Fortunately, she was also a really nice person. So, as you walk toward her with your husband in tow, you decide to bring some style of your own to a gracious introduction: "My dear, this is the person who, as Shakespeare says, used to be the mirror wherein all of us girls did dress ourselves. And, given how great she looks today, the years have not changed a thing."

Other Couplets – *So Smartly Fashionable*

COMMON:

Fashion's standard.

TRANSFORMED:

Fashion's own knight.

~ *Love's Labor's Lost* (I.i.178).

COMMON:

The pride of his country.

TRANSFORMED:

He is the brooch indeed
And gem of all the nation.

~ *Hamlet* (IV.vii.94).

COMMON:

What a smoothie.

TRANSFORMED:

The mirror of all courtesy.

~ *Henry VIII* (II.i.53).

In Praise Of Leadership

WORN-OUT:

What an inspirational leader.

ENERGIZING:

She is a theme of honor and renown,
A spur to valiant and magnanimous deeds.

~ *Troilus and Cressida* (II.ii.199-200).

Face it – some people have such remarkable qualities that they inspire other men and women to do brave and amazing things. While all of your co-workers are talking about what a fabulous boss Sarah is, you'll launch into this quote from the Bard and steal the show.

OTHER COUPLETS – *Because They're Peerless*

COMMON:

The best and brightest.

TRANSFORMED:

The expectation and rose of the fair state.

~ *Hamlet* (III.i.152).

COMMON:

Everyone expects them to succeed.

TRANSFORMED:

The hope and expectation of thy time.

~ *Henry IV, Part One* (III.ii.36).

COMMON:

The very finest we have.

TRANSFORMED:

The choice and master spirits of this age.

~ *Julius Caesar* (III.i.163).

COMMON:

A person of great integrity.

TRANSFORMED:

The theme of honor's tongue.

~ *Henry IV, Part One* (I.i.81).

Cool And Deliberate

INSPIRE NO ONE WITH:

He has a wise courage.

OR IGNITE TRUE ADMIRATION:

'Tis much he dares,
And to that dauntless temper of his mind,
He hath a wisdom that doth guide his valor
To act in safety.
~ *Macbeth* (III.i.49-53).

Do you know one of those rare folks who is skilled at registering disapproval without being hostile or overstepping boundaries? I'm talking about the kind of person who can tell the boss off for a real bonehead decision, yet in such a way as to earn gratitude rather than censure. Yes, such a person is annoying to be around; but here is the perfect quote to make you seem more gracious than you feel.

OTHER COUPLETS – *Steady As She Goes*

COMMON:

Cool as a cucumber.

TRANSFORMED:

Constant in spirit, not swerving with the blood.
~ *Henry V* (II.ii.133).

COMMON:

So composed under pressure.

TRANSFORMED:

Blest are those
Whose blood and judgment are so well commingled,
That they are not a pipe for Fortune's finger
To sound what stop she please.

~ *Hamlet* (III.ii.68-71).

COMMON:

He's mature beyond his years.

TRANSFORMED:

His years but young, but his experience old;
His head unmellowed, but his judgment ripe.

~ *The Two Gentlemen of Verona* (II.iv.69-70).

ELEGANT INSULTS
Beauty's Decline

THIS COULDN'T BE MORE TIRED:

She's really starting to show her years.

OR MORE INCISIVE:

Time's ruin, beauty's wrack, and grim care's reign.

~ *The Rape of Lucrece* (1451).

After a series of tragedies and sorrows, your friend's beautiful face has started to show the telltale signs of wear. When you meet a mutual friend, you can't resist using the above quote; but your innate kindness compels you to conclude with the following: "But I am sure when the calm sets in after all of those storms, she'll look terrific again."

OTHER COUPLETS – *The Glamour Is Fleeting*

COMMON:

She's starting to lose some of her luster.

TRANSFORMED:

Soft, but see, or rather do not see,
My fair rose wither.

~ *Richard II* (V.i.7-8).

COMMON:

She's looking awfully peaked.

TRANSFORMED:

The air hath starved the roses in her cheeks,
and pinched the lily-tincture of her face.

~ *The Two Gentlemen of Verona* (IV.iv.154-155).

Beauty's Deceit

NOTHING SPECIAL HERE:

Her appeal is surface only.

MAGNIFICENT:

O nature, what hadst thou to do in hell
When thou didst bower the spirit of a fiend
In *mortal paradise of such sweet flesh*.

~ *Romeo and Juliet* (III.ii.80-82).

and

O thou weed!
Who art *so lovely fair and smell'st so sweet*,
That the sense aches at thee, would thou hadst
never been born!

~ *Othello* (IV.ii.67-69).

Sadly there are people who do not possess the moral beauty to match their impressive physical endowments. To describe their malignant yet enrapturing power, the use of the above quotes in their entirety is certainly appropriate. But as for me, the italicized portions of both of these quotations are such great descriptions of captivating beauty that I prefer to use them in a positive way. Use "mortal paradise of such sweet flesh" to describe your beloved's face and form and you are not likely to go unappreciated; and the deft use of "so lovely fair and smell'st so sweet, that the sense aches at thee" can only enhance your chances for a romantic conclusion to the evening.

OTHER COUPLETS – *Wickedness Never Looked So Fine*

COMMON:

Her loveliness is just a façade.

TRANSFORMED:

**O that deceit should dwell
In such a gorgeous palace!**

~ *Romeo and Juliet* (III.ii.83-84).

COMMON:

What a charming snake in the grass!

TRANSFORMED:

**O Serpent heart, hid with a flowering face!
Did ever dragon keep so fair a cave?**

~ *Romeo and Juliet* (III.ii.73-74).

COMMON:

He only seems to be both handsome and good.

TRANSFORMED:

Ah! that deceit should steal such gentle shape,
And with a virtuous visor hide deep vice!

~ *Richard III* (II.ii.27-28).

The Obnoxious Male

YOU CAN WEARILY OPINE:

Is there no end to his come-ons?

OR SEIZE THE INITIATIVE:

What, will the line stretch out to the crack of doom?

~ *Macbeth* (IV.i.117).

You and your girlfriends are enjoying a quiet, relaxing drink after work at Marco's Tavern. Unfortunately, for the past fifteen minutes, you have been annoyed past endurance by some of the most obnoxious pick-up verbiage ever to bombard the ears of womankind. Determined to put the creep in his place, you turn to your friends and, loud enough for a certain someone to hear, you say, "What, will this man's line stretch out to the crack of doom?" Of course, the boorish lout may not have a clue as to your Shakespearean brilliance; but this merely confirms the wisdom of your rebuff.

OTHER COUPLETS – *Only One Thing On Their Minds*

COMMON:

Men are beasts.

TRANSFORMED:

They are all but stomachs, and we all but food.

~ *Othello* (III.iv.104).

COMMON:
What a dirty old man.

TRANSFORMED:
The superfluous and lust-dieted man.
~ *King Lear* (IV.i.67).

The Superficial

SO OVERUSED:
What an airhead!

SO RARELY USED:
There can be no kernel in this light nut.
~ *All's Well That Ends Well* (II.v.43).

There's nothing between his or her ears that you can discover. Consequently, this quote will prove quite handy when the notion that a certain person should be put in charge of anything other than watering the plants comes up for discussion.

OTHER COUPLETS – *A Lightness Not To Be Envied*

COMMON:
He's as superficial as he can be.

TRANSFORMED:
The soul of this man is his clothes.
Trust him not in matter of heavy consequence.
~ *All's Well That Ends Well* (II.v.43-45).

COMMON:

He lacks all self-knowledge.

TRANSFORMED:

Yet he hath ever but slenderly known himself.

~ *King Lear* (I.i.293).

The Untrustworthy

SO UNINVENTIVE:

I can't trust you to keep a secret.

SO CUNNING:

For I well believe
Thou wilt not utter what thou dost not know,
And so far will I trust thee.

~ *Henry IV, Part One* (II.iii.110-112).

As the debate rages as to whether or not your co-worker Dudley can be trusted with a critical piece of information, you take the opportunity to remind the group of the last time this congenial dunderhead's noggin possessed key data. After the painful memories of the "leak that cost us a fortune" are recalled in agonizing detail, everyone is quite amenable to the notion that your quote from the Bard will apply to "dear Dudley" quite nicely.

Other Couplets – *You Just Can't Trust Them*

COMMON:

Lying in his/her teeth.

TRANSFORMED:

Falser than vows made in wine.

~ *As You Like It* (III.v.73).

COMMON:

He's such a toady.

TRANSFORMED:

He watered his new plants with dews of flattery.

~ *Coriolanus* (V.vi.23).

COMMON:

You can't find a truthful person.

TRANSFORMED:

To be honest, as this world goes, is to
be one man picked out of ten thousand.

~ *Hamlet* (II.ii.178-179).

The Foolish

LEADEN:

What a bunch of dummies!

AMUSING:

I dare not call them fools; but this I think,
When they are thirsty, fools would fain have drink.

~ *Love's Labor's Lost* (V.ii.371-372).

This is a roundabout way of telling certain folks that they are downright foolish. Of course, if they are really fools, they may not know what you are talking about. And if they're smarter than they seem (like surmising that "fain" means "happily"), they'll pretend that they don't understand your reference or, worse, deliver a swift kick to a certain portion of your anatomy. Of such dilemmas are Shakespearean champions born.

Other Couplets – *Wisdom Is Not Their Thing*

COMMON:

You're old enough to know better.

TRANSFORMED:

How ill white hairs becomes a fool and jester!

~ *Henry IV, Part Two* (V.v.48).

and

Thou shouldst not have been old till thou hadst been wise.

~ *King Lear* (I.v.44).

COMMON:

What a trusting fool.

TRANSFORMED:

[He] is of a free and open nature,
That thinks men honest that but seem to be so,
And will as tenderly be led by the nose
As asses are.

~ *Othello* (I.iii.399-402).

The Puffed-Up

BARELY BELIEVABLE:

He'll get his comeuppance.

BEYOND ALL DOUBT:

For it shall come to pass
That every braggart shall be found an ass.

~ *All's Well That Ends Well* (IV.iii.335-336).

A certain arrogant fellow of your acquaintance is in full bluster again. You turn to your companion and utter the above words with just the right amount of disdain dripping from your lips.

OTHER COUPLETS –
They're So Pleased With Themselves

COMMON:

What a pompous ass.

TRANSFORMED:

How now, my sweet creature of bombast.

~ *Henry IV, Part One* (II.iv.326-327).

COMMON:

I sure did great work.

TRANSFORMED:

Now hath my soul brought forth her prodigy.

~ *Richard II* (II.ii.64).

COMMON:

He loves the sound of his own voice.

TRANSFORMED:

One who the music of his own vain tongue
Doth ravish like enchanting harmony.

~ *Love's Labor's Lost* (I.i.166-167).

The Long-Winded

ALL TOO FAMILIAR:
What a windbag!

DELIGHTFULLY DIFFERENT:
Here will be an old abusing of God's patience and the King's English.
~ *The Merry Wives of Windsor* (I.iv.4-6).

The gasbag who has bored the pants off you and your co-workers countless times is about to crank it up again. And, as always, he'll be doing inexcusable damage to the English language in the process. The Bard has his number.

OTHER COUPLETS –
They Can't Stop Flapping Their Gums

COMMON:
He can't stop talking.

TRANSFORMED:
A gentleman … that loves to hear himself talk, and will speak more in a minute than he will stand to in a month.
~ *Romeo and Juliet* (II.iv.147-149).

COMMON:
What a chatterbox.

TRANSFORMED:
Fie, what a spendthrift is he of his tongue!
~ *The Tempest* (II.i.24).

The Sharp-Tongued

TOO BLUNT:

You've got quite the nasty tongue.

JUST RIGHT:

The world's large tongue
Proclaims you for a man replete with mocks.

~ *Love's Labor's Lost* (V.ii.842-843).

How can you not love "the world's large tongue proclaims." This gem can preface all sorts of things, such as "that you're a fool for love," or "that he's a complete cad," or "that she's a total loser." Of course, you can just as easily place complimentary things after "proclaims"; but it's not nearly as much fun.

OTHER COUPLETS – *Biting Words*

COMMON:

Cut the bull.

TRANSFORMED:

More matter with less art.

~ *Hamlet* (II.ii.95).

COMMON:

Let's stop this bitter quarreling.

TRANSFORMED:

Now for the love of Love and her soft hours,
Let's not confound the time with conference harsh.

~ *Antony and Cleopatra* (I.i.44-45).

NOT SO ELEGANT INSULTS
An Array Of Faults

SO CRASS:

What a blubber-butt!

SO CLEVERLY CRASS:

[He] lards the lean earth as he walks along.

~ *Henry IV, Part One* (II.ii.109).

Obviously you could use this quote in a very mean way to describe an exceptionally plump person as he or she ambles along. But you are better than that. Instead you choose to use the above quote to comment on that otherwise delightful person you know who is forever preoccupied with a tenth of a pound. Try this: "She has a great figure; but to hear her talk you would think, as Shakespeare says, that she 'lards the lean earth' as she walks along."

OTHER COUPLETS – *So Much To Criticize*

COMMON:

The man is a coward.

TRANSFORMED:

[He has] no more man's blood in his belly that will sup a flea.

~ *Love's Labor's Lost* (V.ii.691-692).

COMMON:

He's such a wimp.

TRANSFORMED:

A milksop, one that never in his life
Felt so much cold as over shoes in snow.

~ *Richard III* (V.iii.325-326).

COMMON:

What a terrible voice.

TRANSFORMED:

O tax not so bad a voice
To slander music any more than once.

~ *Much Ado About Nothing* (II.iii.44-45).

A Pathetic Display

NO EDGE:

Such a bozo.

WELL-SHARPENED:

And much fool may you find... even to the world's
pleasure and the increase of laughter.

~ *All's Well That Ends Well* (II.iv.35-37).

He thinks he's so charming as he persists in his feeble attempts to make amorous conquests. You can't resist employing the above quote, as you concur with a friend that the man is an ass. Perhaps you will do the guy a favor and spell out in no uncertain terms why there is always a pronounced increase in snickering when he breezes through a party.

Other Couplets – *Nothing Good To Say*

COMMON:

He always gives me indigestion.

TRANSFORMED:

I never can see him but I am heart-burned an hour after.

~ *Much Ado About Nothing* (II.i.3-4).

COMMON:

You're completely worthless.

TRANSFORMED:

You are not worth the dust which the rude wind Blows in your face!

~ *King Lear* (IV.ii.30-31).

COMMON:

I wouldn't trust him as far as I can throw him.

TRANSFORMED:

I will trust [him] as I will adders fanged.

~ *Hamlet* (III.iv.203).

COMMON:

What a loser.

TRANSFORMED:

Wherein is he good, but to taste sack and drink it?
wherein neat and cleanly, but to carve a capon
and eat it?
wherein cunning, but in craft?
wherein crafty, but in villainy?
wherein villainous, but in all things?
wherein worthy, but in nothing?

~ Henry IV, Part One (II.iv.455-459).

[Note: Sack = white wine with brandy added – today's sherry.]

COMMON:

Get a load of those outfits.

TRANSFORMED:

What are these
So withered and so wild in their attire,
That look not like the inhabitants of the earth,
And yet are on it.

~ Macbeth (I.iii.39-42).

CHAPTER 3.
MARRIAGE, FAMILY AND FRIENDS –
Not Another Comfort Like To This

MARRIAGE

Whether in Elizabethan times or our own, the subject of marriage has always been the occasion for sweeping hyperbole regarding its marvels and, occasionally, equally extravagant denunciation. No one knew this better than Shakespeare. His delight in tweaking the nose of marital expectation seems to be matched only by the pleasure he takes in ensuring that the matrimonial cynic eats his well-deserved ration of connubial crow. Bon appetit!

Taking The Plunge

DIRECT BUT WOODEN:
Breaking my promise will be well worth it.

SMOOTH AND CLEVER:
What fool is not so wise
To lose an oath to win a paradise?
~ *Love's Labor's Lost* (IV.iii.70-71).

You are tired of people reminding you of your longstanding promise never to "put a ring though your nose." That was before you met the fabulous person who has become the love of your life. Now you know better and, after your friends have met this incredible person, you have the perfect explanation for your ardent recantation: "I know my former remarks make me look foolish; but now that you have met her/him, can you blame me for following Shakespeare's advice, 'What fool is not so wise/To lose an oath to win a paradise.'"

OTHER COUPLETS – *You Know When To Say "Yes"*

COMMON:

I never thought I would get married.

TRANSFORMED:

No, the world must be peopled.
When I said I would die a bachelor, I did not think I should live till I were married.

~ *Much Ado About Nothing* (II.iii.242).

COMMON:

The urge to merge.

TRANSFORMED:

Man hath his desires; and as pigeons bill, so wedlock would be nibbling.

~ *As You Like It* (III.iii.83).

Connubial Bliss

INSIST WITH FOREBODING:

I'll never be happier than today.

OR EMBRACE THE MOMENT:

If it were now to die,
'Twere now to be most happy; for I fear
My soul hath her content so absolute
That not another comfort like to this
Succeeds in unknown fate.

~ *Othello* (II.i.189-193).

Your marriage is terrific and you're not afraid to show it. After a wonderful anniversary evening, you leave a card on your spouse's pillow. Changing "fear" to "think," you pen the above quote and the following sentiment: "So many moments with you seem like the peak moment of my life. Last night was another one." And don't worry about that "unknown fate" reference. Unlike Othello, who spoke these words about the lovely but doomed Desdemona, you know you've got the best deal in town.

OTHER COUPLETS –
You Can Never Get Too Much Sugar

COMMON:

Let's cuddle.

TRANSFORMED:

Come, madam wife, sit by my side, and let
the world slip, we shall ne'er be younger.

~ *The Taming of the Shrew* (Induction.ii.142-144).

COMMON:

How about a little smooch.

TRANSFORMED:

My lips, two blushing pilgrims, ready stand
To smooth that rough touch with a tender kiss.
~ *Romeo and Juliet* (I.v.95-96).

A Gem Of A Spouse

TRUE BUT HUMDRUM:

She's utterly captivating.

TRUE AND BREATHTAKING:

A wife
Whose beauty did astonish the survey
Of richest eyes, whose words all ears took captive,
Whose dear perfection hearts that scorn'd to serve
Humbly call'd mistress.
~ *All's Well That Ends Well* (V.iii.15-19).

This is a truly lovely paean of praise to a connubial partner. It's the perfect quote for an anniversary card. Begin with something like this: "I am at a loss for words to describe how much you mean to me. Fortunately, Shakespeare has said it for me." Then you inscribe the above quote and prove beyond doubt that you are indeed one classy fellow.

OTHER COUPLETS – *No Praise Is Too High*

COMMON:

You just can't say enough good things about her.

TRANSFORMED:

For thou shalt find she will outstrip all praise
And make it halt behind her.

~ The Tempest (IV.i.10-11).

[Note: Outstrip = exceed; halt = hobble.]

COMMON:

I don't deserve her.

TRANSFORMED:

O ye gods!
Render me worthy of this noble wife!

~ Julius Caesar (II.i.303).

COMMON:

She's worthy of my devotion.

TRANSFORMED:

Wise, fair, and true,
Shall she be placed in my constant soul.

~ The Merchant of Venice (II.vi.56-57).

Expectations And The Lowering Thereof

GO PHILOSOPHICALLY FLAT:

Expectation is greater than realization.

OR HIT JUST THE RIGHT NOTE:

All things that are,
Are with more spirit chased than enjoyed.

~ The Merchant of Venice (II.vi.12-13).

"I'm afraid reality has not met expectations," your friend confides, as she bemoans the fact that her marriage is not all sweetness and light. "The truth is that my marriage has gotten a bit dull." "It only goes to prove," you opine, "that Shakespeare was right when he said that 'all things are with more spirit chased than enjoyed.'"

Other Couplets –
So You Can Depress Every Newlywed In Town

COMMON:

I just can't trust her.

TRANSFORMED:

O curse of marriage!
That we can call these delicate creatures ours,
And not their appetites!
~ *Othello* (III.iii.268-270).

COMMON:

Just wait until she has that ring on her finger.

TRANSFORMED:

Maids are May when they are maids,
but the sky changes when they are wives.
~ *As You Like It* (IV.i.148-149).

Yes, Dear

SURRENDER MEEKLY:
Yes, honey, of course I'll go.

OR SURRENDER WITH STYLE:
I will live in thy heart, die in thy lap, and be buried in thy eyes; and moreover I will go with thee to thy uncle's.
~ *Much Ado About Nothing* (V.ii.102-104).

Any dolt can say, "Yes, honey, of course I'll go," and then proceed to visit an annoying relative. Only an individual of your sophistication can use the opportunity to sermonize about the meaning of your marriage, quote the Bard, and then proceed to visit that same annoying relative. The difference is incalculable.

OTHER COUPLETS –
There Is No Shame In Yielding

COMMON:
Only for her would I give up my freedom.

TRANSFORMED:
But that I love the gentle Desdemona,
I would not my unhoused free condition
Put into circumscription and confine
For the sea's worth.
~ *Othello* (I.ii.25-28).

COMMON:

We all succumb in the end.

TRANSFORMED:

In time the savage bull doth bear the yoke.

~ *Much Ado About Nothing* (I.i.261).

Marital Cynics

SAY IT WARILY:

Young fellows should be careful about tying the knot.

OR DARE TO BE FORTHRIGHT:

A young man married is a man that's marr'd.

~ *All's Well That Ends Well* (II.iii.298).

It is impossible to conceive of an appropriate use for this disgraceful sentiment. It is presented here only to roundly condemn it and to assure my own dear wife of my eternal love.

OTHER COUPLETS – *If You Insist On Being Snide*

COMMON:

Some people should never get married.

TRANSFORMED:

Many a good hanging prevents a bad marriage.

~ *Twelfth Night* (I.v.19).

COMMON:

In the grip of second thoughts.

TRANSFORMED:

Who woo'd in haste, and means to wed at leisure.

~ *The Taming of the Shrew* (III.ii.11).

COMMON:

We will never find peace again.

TRANSFORMED:

Undone, and forfeited to cares for ever!

~ *All's Well That Ends Well* (II.iii.267).

COMMON:

When we're in love, we can be so foolish.

TRANSFORMED:

**To be wise and love
Exceeds men's might.**

~ *Troilus and Cressida* (III.ii.156-157).

FAMILY

Shakespeare was quite familiar with the joys and hazards of familial relationships. He didn't need a modern course in "family dynamics" to plumb the complexities thereof, and all you will need is his provocative imagery to dazzle the crowd. Our tone here is essentially light-hearted. The King Lears of this world may be less amused.

Parental Exasperation

TRY THE DIVINE PATIENCE:
Good God, this kid needs help!

OR PIQUE THE DIVINE CURIOSITY:
O you kind gods!
Cure this great breach in his abused nature.
~ *King Lear* (IV.vii.14-15).

Your daughter or son has just returned home with the most repulsive hairdo imaginable. Don't rant and rave; don't crassly suggest that a bag should be placed over the offender's head. These are the comments of the unenlightened. No, you will merely turn heavenward and loudly pray the above quote, with gender adjustment as required. Is there any doubt your child will respect you for your erudition and immediately vow never again to upset you with such thoughtless behavior?

OTHER COUPLETS –
More Ways To Express Your Annoyance

COMMON:
Where's that idiot?

TRANSFORMED:
Where is this rash and most unfortunate man?
~ *Othello* (V.ii.283).

[Note: Feel free to revise to "young man" or "young woman,"
or simply "child," as appropriate.]

COMMON:
> *Outrageous behavior.*

TRANSFORMED:
> **Bold and saucy wrongs.**
> ~ *Othello* (I.i.128).

Tough Love

HOW CRUDE:
> *Beat it kids!*

HOW STYLISHLY CRUDE:
> **Hence! home, you idle creatures, get you home!**
> ~ *Julius Caesar* (I.i.1).

These are the perfect words to use as you send home the teenage friends of your son or daughter prior to the family dinner. You'll find that kicking the annoying urchins out of the house has never been sweeter.

OTHER COUPLETS – *You've Got To Hang Tough*

COMMON:
> *Watch your mouth.*

TRANSFORMED:
> **Mend your speech a little,**
> **Lest you may mar your fortunes.**
> ~ *King Lear* (I.i.94).

COMMON:

The rules of the house.

TRANSFORMED:

The needful bits and curbs to headstrong steeds.

~ *Measure for Measure* (I.iii.20).

COMMON:

This will keep her in line.

TRANSFORMED:

And thus I'll curb her mad and headstrong humor.

~ *The Taming of the Shrew* (IV.i.209).

COMMON:

You'll thank me later for saying what you need to hear.

TRANSFORMED:

Better a little chiding than a great deal of heartbreak.

~ *The Merry Wives of Windsor* (V.iii.9-10).

The Scheming Never Ends

PERSUADE NO ONE:

Let's put on an act.

OR IMPRESS MIGHTILY:

**[Let's] play one scene
Of excellent dissembling, and let it look
Like perfect honor.**

~ *Antony and Cleopatra* (I.iii.78-80).

It's off to another family dinner and yet another evening of Uncle Bill's offensive remarks, Aunt Miranda's repulsive politics, and Grandpa Charlie's thoroughly nauseating jokes. Yes, you'll go and, yes, you'll succeed in not embarrassing your spouse with your boorish reactions. But, before you go, you will not resist a rather pompous sweep of the hand as you cite the above quote, taking care to change "perfect honor" to "perfect sweetness," and looking truly scornful while you say it. Gad, it's great to be self-righteous.

OTHER COUPLETS – *Necessary Ploys And Strategies*

COMMON:
> *We can't stop plotting for a moment.*

TRANSFORMED:
> **Every minute now**
> **Should be the father of some stratagem.**
> ~ *Henry IV, Part Two* (I.i.7-8).

COMMON:
> *For now I'll pretend to put up with your nonsense.*

TRANSFORMED:
> **I know you all, and will awhile uphold**
> **The unyoked humor of your idleness.**
> ~ *Henry IV, Part One* (I.ii.195-196).

COMMON:

To discover the extent of this wrongdoing.

TRANSFORMED:

To sound the depth of this knavery.

~ *The Taming of the Shrew* (V.i.137).

Kids Will Be Kids

PRATFALL WITH:

What a clown!

OR BE IN CHARGE OF THE CIRCUS:

Why, what a madcap hath heaven lent us here!

~ *King John* (I.i.84).

Your child's report card tells more than you care to know about the value of the so-called study sessions with friends. Your remarks may well feature language of a less elegant nature, but you begin with the above quote before proceeding to a discussion of where your little darling will be spending the next two months after school. Something tells me it won't be "studying" with friends.

OTHER COUPLETS – *They Just Can't Help It*

COMMON:

Boys with no thought of ever growing up.

TRANSFORMED:

Two lads that thought there were no more…
But such a day to-morrow as to-day,
And to be boy eternal.

~ *The Winter's Tale* (I.ii.63-64).

COMMON:
Preoccupied with their pleasures.

TRANSFORMED:
All knit up
In their distractions.
~ *The Tempest* (III.iii.89-90).

FRIENDS

To Shakespeare, friendship was an essential aspect of living. The loyalty and the treachery of friends figured prominently in his plays. Focusing exclusively on the positive, this brief section poignantly affirms the inestimable value of having loving friends in your life.

A Special Joy

BORE THEM ALL:
There's nothing more important than friends.

OR GET THEM THINKING:
I count myself in nothing else so happy
As in a soul rememb'ring my good friends.
~ *Richard II* (II.iii.46-47).

Your friends have given you the most rousing birthday celebration of all time. Now the din of what seems like a thousand voices is heard as the words "speech, speech" reverberate. You've got the perfect beginning with this quote, and there won't be a dry eye in the house when you're done.

OTHER COUPLETS – *Few Things Are More Precious*

COMMON:

I bared my soul to him.

TRANSFORMED:

**[I] made him my book, wherein my soul recorded
The history of all her secret thoughts.**

~ *Richard III* (III.v.27-28).

COMMON:

You're my confidant.

TRANSFORMED:

**Thou know'st no less but all. I have unclasp'd
To thee the book even of my secret soul.**

~ *Twelfth Night* (I.iv.13-14).

COMMON:

We're going to share everything.

TRANSFORMED:

**By and by thy bosom shall partake
The secrets of my heart.**

~ *Julius Caesar* (II.i.305-306).

COMMON:

I'll never stop being grateful for your help and friendship.

TRANSFORMED:

**To be more thankful to thee shall be my study, and
my profit therein the heaping friendships.**

~ *The Winter's Tale* (IV.ii.18-20).

COMMON:

I treasure the friend with a calm disposition.

TRANSFORMED:

Give me that man
That is not passion's slave, and I will wear him
In my heart's core, ay, in my heart of heart,
As I do thee.

~ *Hamlet* (III.ii.71-74).

CHAPTER 4.
THE WORK-A-DAY WORLD –
So Foul And Fair A Day

Work, work, work – that's all you seem to do. Up until now, when you wanted to complain about your job, whine about your evaluation, make a snide remark about your supervisor, and share with your co-workers some salacious gossip – you know, the basics of a happy work life – you had to rely on the same stash of boring cliches that every one else employs. But now you will possess a veritable treasure-trove of clever turns of phrase to dazzle your co-workers. Be assured that the old briar patch will never be quite the same once you start to shake things up with some Shakespearean sleight-of-tongue.

Wise Office Strategies

LAG BEHIND WITH:
> *Easy does it.*

OR MAKE PLODDING ALONG SEEM COOL:
> **Wisely and slow, they stumble that run fast.**
> ~ *Romeo and Juliet* (II.iii.94).

As you calmly and unhurriedly go about your assigned tasks at work, it amuses you to observe your co-workers scurrying about like mice. Clearly they are violating the wise principle of energy conservation that the above quote illustrates. You enjoy uttering these immortal words of the Bard to all about you as the work-a-day world proceeds. But, alas, the day takes on a much darker tone when you experience the rather pointed retort of your boss: "Smartly and quick. They get fired who run slow." You immediately rethink your position and begin to hustle your behind, wisely concluding that Friar Lawrence, the clergyman who spoke these words in *Romeo and Juliet*, had guaranteed employment and you don't.

OTHER COUPLETS – *You Need To Be Savvy*

COMMON:

I'm not saying a thing.

TRANSFORMED:

**I will be the pattern of all patience,
I will say nothing.**

~ *King Lear* (III.ii.37).

COMMON:

She's as sly as a fox.

TRANSFORMED:

She is cunning past man's thought.

~ *Antony and Cleopatra* (I.ii.145).

Wily Office Strategies

NOTHING SPECIAL:

All thought, no action.

DISTINCTIVE:

Function
Is smothered in surmise, and nothing is
But what is not.

~ *Macbeth* (I.iii.140).

When it comes to day-to-day pragmatic operations, the management team at your workplace seems to be about as useful as a worn-out sock. Rather than focus on practical issues, their heads are always in the clouds (their "function is smothered in surmise"). It's as if the only thing that is real to them is what might be in the future (thus "nothing is but what is not"). You just can't resist laying this quote on your fellow co-workers, in suitably outraged tones. Of course, without an explanation by you, they won't have a clue as to what you are saying. But then they will think of you as a brilliant Shakespearean scholar and not as some loser who couldn't manage to make it onto the management team in the first place.

OTHER COUPLETS – *They Think They're So Clever*

COMMON:

What an ass kisser.

TRANSFORMED:

What a candy deal of courtesy
This fawning greyhound then did proffer me!

~ *Henry IV, Part One* (I.iii.251-252).

COMMON:

No one is safe from his greedy claws.

TRANSFORMED:

No man's pie is freed
From his ambitious finger.

~ *Henry VIII* (I.i.52-53).

Co-Worker Flaws

HARSH SELF-FLAGELLATION:

It's no one's fault but our own.

THOUGHTFUL SELF-EXAMINATION:

Men at some time are masters of their fates;
The fault, dear Brutus, is not in our stars,
But in ourselves, that we are underlings.

~ *Julius Caesar* (I.ii.139-141).

If your co-worker complains one more time about how he or she has gotten a bum rap in yet another round of promotions, you're going to scream. What you want to say is "Try studying for the supervisor's exam for a change, stupid." But, instead, you decide to lay some class on the classless boor by citing the above quote, with appropriate gender adjustment. Then you add, "So try studying next time, knucklehead." Much better.

OTHER COUPLETS – *Some Changes Are In Order*

COMMON:

It's great that they're open to changing their ways.

TRANSFORMED:

Happy are they that hear their detractions and can put them to mending.

~ *Much Ado About Nothing* (II.iii.229-230).

COMMON:

Let's hope you'll have the skill to convince him.

TRANSFORMED:

Well, God give thee the spirit of persuasion and him the ears of profiting.

~ *Henry IV, Part One* (I.ii.152-153).

Comeuppance Time

OLD AS THE HILLS:

They'll get theirs someday.

OLD AND STILL FRESH:

And thus the whirligig of time brings in his revenges.

~ *Twelfth Night* (V.i.376-377).

Oh, how sweet it is! The obnoxious creep who, as your supervisor, has been a pain in your behind for years is in the process of getting a well-earned comeuppance from an even more obnoxious superior. And you're enjoying every minute, as you turn to your co-worker to offer some profound Shakespearean commentary.

OTHER COUPLETS – *You're Getting Quite Concerned*

COMMON:

You paid the price for recklessness.

TRANSFORMED:

This is the fruit of rashness!

~ *Richard III* (II.i.135).

COMMON:

What goes around, comes around.

TRANSFORMED:

The wheel is come full circle.

~ *King Lear* (V.iii.175).

COMMON:

I lost perspective and now I'm paying for it.

TRANSFORMED:

**Had I but served my God with half the zeal
I served my king, He would not in mine age
Have left me naked to mine enemies.**

~ *Henry VIII* (III.ii.455-457).

COMMON:

Sound advice, but too late to help.

TRANSFORMED:

**That comfort comes too late,
'Tis like a pardon after execution.**

~ *Henry VIII* (IV.ii.120-121).

COMMON:
You got me. I have to admit it.

TRANSFORMED:
A touch, a touch, I do confess.
~ *Hamlet* (V.ii.286).

and

A hit, a very palpable hit.
~ *Hamlet* (V.ii.281).

COMMON:
I got my butt kicked tonight.

TRANSFORMED:
I have been tonight exceedingly well cudgeled.
~ *Othello* (II.iii.365-366).

Workday Anxiety

DUTY AS PROSE:
I feel so weighed down with responsibilities.

DUTY AS POETRY:
So shaken as we are, so wan with care.
~ *Henry* IV, Part One (I.i.1).

This week your job has been a real drag. So when someone asks you how things are going, you respond with a hammy sigh and the above quote.

Other Couplets – *You've Got To Watch Your Back*

COMMON:

You can never relax when you're on top.

TRANSFORMED:

Uneasy lies the head that wears a crown.

~ *Henry* IV, Part Two (III.i.31).

COMMON:

Keep your eyes peeled.

TRANSFORMED:

Be wary then, best safety lies in fear.

~ *Hamlet* (I.iii.43).

COMMON:

Like crabs in a barrel.

TRANSFORMED:

Had you an eye behind you, you might see more detraction at your heels than fortunes before you.

~ *Twelfth Night* (II.v.136-138).

Deception All Around

MAKE THEIR EYES ROLL WITH:

You can't judge a book by its cover.

OR GIVE THEM A REASON TO FOCUS:

When devils will the blackest sins put on, They do suggest at first with heavenly shows.

~ *Othello* (II.iii.351-352).

In the guise of a thoroughly pleasant fellow, a serpent has slithered into the office and is now in line to take the job you have wanted for years. With his fancy clothes, shiny MBA, and revoltingly toothy smile, he has clearly won over all of your co-workers. "Don't be deceived," you say (objectivity is one of your great virtues), as you proceed to employ the above quote with all of the fanfare you can muster.

OTHER COUPLETS – *Someone's Snookering Someone*

COMMON:

> *I put on a good front.*

TRANSFORMED:

> **I am not merry; but I do beguile**
> **The thing I am by seeming otherwise.**
> ~ *Othello* (II.i.122-123).

COMMON:

> *They're all snakes in the grass.*

TRANSFORMED:

> **Your Grace attended to their sugared words,**
> **But looked not on the poison of their hearts.**
> ~ *Richard* III (III.i.13-14).

COMMON:

> *Many a hypocrite can quote the Bible.*

TRANSFORMED:

> **The devil can cite Scripture for his purpose.**
> ~ *The Merchant of Venice* (I.iii.98).

Praising Exceptional Work

HOW TEDIOUS:

He sure looks good by comparison.

HOW INTERESTING:

**How he glisters
Through my rust!**

~ *The Winter's Tale* (III.ii.170-171).

She has amazing skills and everyone knows it – everyone, of course, but the boss, who only has praise for himself. So there's no surprise that her presentation at work makes his look like gibberish. You can't resist leaning over and whispering to your colleagues, "Oh how she glisters through his rust."

OTHER COUPLETS – *Acclaim That Is Noteworthy*

COMMON:

He's far exceeded expectations.

TRANSFORMED:

**He hath borne himself beyond the promise
of his age.**

~ *Much Ado About Nothing* (I.i.13-14).

COMMON:

Beautifully done.

TRANSFORMED:

**O, your desert speaks loud.
... It deserves with characters of brass
A forted residence against the tooth of time
And razure of oblivion.**

~ *Measure for Measure* (V.i.9-13).

82

COMMON:
A bolt of inspiration.

TRANSFORMED:
The flash and outbreak of a fiery mind.
~ *Hamlet* (II.i.33).

Embracing Contradictions

FORGO THIS TIRED MIXTURE:
This day has been a mixed bag.

AND TRY THIS CLEVER CONCOCTION:
So foul and fair a day I have not seen.
~ *Macbeth* (I.iii.38).

It's been raining for three days, your St. Bernard has diarrhea, and your spouse can't stand the sight of you – but you just got a big fat raise.

OTHER COUPLETS – *For "Both/And" Thinkers*

COMMON:
Pretend it doesn't hurt.

TRANSFORMED:
The robbed that smiles steals something from the thief.
~ *Othello* (I.iii. 208).

COMMON:
Being smart is good; being lucky is better.

TRANSFORMED:
Fortune brings in some boats that are not steered.
~ *Cymbeline* (IV.iii.46).

Mentoring With Care

JOIN THE CROWD:

Thanks for the advice – I'll follow it.

OR IMPRESS WITH SOMETHING SPECIAL:

I will stoop and humble my intents
To your well-practiced wise directions.

~ Henry IV, Part Two (V.ii.120-121).

You've just received really good counsel from a senior co-worker and you know full well that you better follow it. So, rejecting the shopworn "thank you" that everyone else would choose, you send an e-mail featuring the above quote, thereby conclusively proving that you were worth the trouble of being mentored in the first place.

OTHER COUPLETS – *Let The Education Begin*

COMMON:

I'll continue to be your tutor.

TRANSFORMED:

I have begun to plant thee, and will labor
To make thee full of growing.

~ Macbeth (I.iv.28-29).

COMMON:

Listen to me; I know what the deal is.

TRANSFORMED:

Bosom up my counsel,
You'll find it wholesome.

~ *Henry VIII* (I.i.112-113).

COMMON:

My advice is simple: work within your capacity.

TRANSFORMED:

I should not urge thy duty past thy might.

~ *Julius Caesar* (IV.iii.261).

Chapter 5.
Recreation And Travel –
The Pert And Nimble Spirit

Recreation

Although it will never cease to be a source of astonishment to some folks, not everyone in this world is enamored of the sporting life. But for those whose nostrils flare at the very mention of competition, who yearn to dole out a full measure of just desserts to their sportive combatants, we offer these rapier thrusts from the Bard.

Entering The Fray

MERIT A SNEER:
> *My team is certain to win.*

OR EARN THEIR ADMIRATION:
> **All friends shall taste**
> **The wages of their virtue, and all foes**
> **The cup of their deservings.**

~ *King Lear* (V.iii.303-305).

As you charge onto the soccer field, you loudly proclaim this fearless quote. Now it's true that your team usually stinks up the place, and a lesser quote master might shy away from such bold optimism. But you are a Shakespearean quote master. You are a winner whether or not your team actually "tastes the wages" of victory. And you'll keep telling yourself that, yes you will.

OTHER COUPLETS – *For The Battle-Tested You*

COMMON:

Here's hoping you prevail.

TRANSFORMED:

Upon your sword
Sit laurel victory, and smooth success
Be strewed before your feet!
~ *Antony and Cleopatra* (I.iii.99-101).

and

Fortune and victory sit on thy helm!
~ *Richard III* (V.iii.79).

COMMON:

May fortune smile on you.

TRANSFORMED:

[May] the fair goddess Fortune
Fall deep in love with thee.
~ *Coriolanus* (I.v.20-21).

COMMON:

I can see you're ready for some action.

TRANSFORMED:

**I see you stand like greyhounds in the slips,
Straining upon the start.**

~ *Henry V* (III.i.31-32).

COMMON:

Let's fight smartly not rashly.

TRANSFORMED:

**Like Romans, neither foolish in our stands
Nor cowardly in retire.**

~ *Coriolanus* (I.vi.2).

[Note: Change "Romans" to your champions of choice.]

COMMON:

The best way to stop a bully is with a bigger bully.

TRANSFORMED:

Lions make leopards tame.

~ *Richard II* (I.i.174).

When The Battle Is Over

ROLL SNAKE EYES:

Someone eventually will triumph.

OR MAKE THE DICE SING:

**Then, in a moment, Fortune shall cull forth
Out of one side her happy minion.**

~ *King John* (II.i.391-392).

You are reporting back to the group with a blow-by-blow description of how the team won the contest in the final seconds. Your narrative smoothly rises to this crescendo: "The match could have gone either way. The audience held its collective breath. Then, as Shakespeare said, 'in a moment fortune culled forth out of one side her happy minion.' In short, the point and match were ours."

OTHER COUPLETS – *For The Warrior In You*

COMMON:

We won!

TRANSFORMED:

Victory sits on our helms.

~ *Richard III* (V.iii.351).

COMMON:

When the battle has been decided.

TRANSFORMED:

When the hurly-burly's done,
When the battle's lost and won.

~ *Macbeth* (I.i.3-4).

COMMON:

We beat ourselves.

TRANSFORMED:

England, that was wont to conquer others
Hath made a shameful conquest of itself.

~ *Richard II* (II.i.65-66).

[Note: Change "England" to the name of your team.]

COMMON:
A soldier's glory is fleeting.

TRANSFORMED:
O, withered is the garland of the war.
~ Antony and Cleopatra (IV.xv.64).

To Have What It Takes

SO PREDICTABLE:
He's at the peak of his powers.

SO STIMULATING:
The very May-morn of his youth,
Ripe for exploits and mighty enterprises.
~ Henry V (I.ii.120-121).

The white water rapids are beckoning. You and your group of stalwart friends are eager for the challenge. But you can't resist the opportunity to rib your best friend back home for his or her couch potato temperament. So, before you dip your canoe into the rapids, you take a picture of the brave crew and then attach it to an e-mail that reads: "Here we are in the very May-morn of our youth, ripe for exploits and mighty enterprises. By the way did you receive the rocking chair and slippers I sent you?"

Other Couplets – *You're Ready To Handle Anything*

COMMON:

You're on top of the world.

TRANSFORMED:

There thou stand'st, a breathing valiant man,
Of an invincible unconquered spirit.

~ *Henry VI, Part One* (IV.ii.31-32).

COMMON:

A guy that has it all.

TRANSFORMED:

A combination and a form indeed,
Where every god did seem to set his seal
To give the world assurance of a man.

~ *Hamlet* (III.iv.60-62).

Focusing Your Energy

EMBARRASS YOURSELF WITH:

I can't wait to take my revenge.

OR GIVE REVENGE SOME STYLE:

All studies here I solemnly defy,
Save how to gall and pinch this Bolingbroke.

~ *Henry IV, Part One* (I.iii.228-229).

You've just been thoroughly humiliated in your favorite sport by someone who doesn't know the meaning of the words "gracious winner." Your otherwise tranquil and kind heart is now filled with sweet revenge. When someone asks you how you are going to handle this most recent indignity, you respond with the above quote, changing Bolingbroke to the name of your nemesis, for example, Charles, Kathy or Bill. Of course, you could rise above such pettiness, but then you wouldn't be able to use this deliciously wicked quote.

Other Couplets – *You're Totally Consumed*

COMMON:
Get yourself psyched-up.

TRANSFORMED:
Put fire in your heart, and brimstone in your liver.
~ *Twelfth Night* (III.ii.20-21).

COMMON:
Nothing can stop me now.

TRANSFORMED:
Nothing that can be can come between me and the full prospect of my hopes.
~ *Twelfth Night* (III.iv.81-82).

Travel

How many times have you sat down to write a postcard from your vacation paradise? Your pen begins to scrawl the familiar "having a wonderful time, wish you were here," and then you groan under the weight of your own banality. Well, groan no more; dispense with the trite and the commonplace. Once you've put these Shakespearean quotes in your travel portfolio, you're sure to capture the attention of the folks back home. After all, the true purpose of travel postcards is to make your friends green with envy.

Kicking Back And Relaxing

NO ONE'S INTEREST IS PIQUED:

I'm just going to chill out.

NOW THERE'S ENVY ALL AROUND:

Merrily, merrily shall I live now,
Under the blossom that hangs on the bough.

~ *The Tempest* (V.i.93-94).

The place is a lounge lizard's dream. You have absolutely nothing to do but soak up some rays. The postcard features swaying palm trees and a gorgeous sunset. The quote is from Shakespeare. The pleasure is all yours.

OTHER COUPLETS – *You Need To Take It Easy*

COMMON:

This place is really relaxing.

TRANSFORMED:

This castle hath a pleasant seat, the air
Nimbly and sweetly recommends itself
Unto our gentle senses.

~ *Macbeth* (I.vi.1-3).

[Note: Change "castle" to your preferred place of enjoyment.]

COMMON:

How should we spend our free time enjoyably?

TRANSFORMED:

How shall we beguile
The lazy time, if not with some delight?

~ *A Midsummer Night's Dream* (V.i.40-41).

COMMON:
Peaceful and undisturbed.

TRANSFORMED:
Shut up
In measureless content.
~ *Macbeth* (II.i.16-17).

COMMON:
At last I have some time for quiet contemplation.

TRANSFORMED:
Now my soul hath elbow room.
~ *King John* (V.vii.28).

Diving Into Pleasure

COULD YOU BE MORE TRITE:
Nothing compares with doing this.

OR MORE PROFOUND:
Kingdoms are clay... the nobleness of life
Is to do thus [they embrace].
~ *Antony and Cleopatra* (I.i.35-37).

Those gorgeous European castles are perfect for the effect you're looking for. While a helpful fellow tourist takes the picture, you plant a big smooch on your traveling companion, and then promptly e-mail the digital evidence to a long list of potentially envious friends. You add the following words: "These castles are great but the extracurriculars are even better. As the Bard said, 'Kingdoms are clay, the nobleness of life is to do thus.'"

Other Couplets – *It's Time To Have Some Fun*

COMMON:

Just go and do your own thing.

TRANSFORMED:

Each man to what sport and revels his addiction leads him.

~ *Othello* (II.ii.5-6).

COMMON:

Let's party.

TRANSFORMED:

Awake the pert and nimble spirit of mirth.

~ *A Midsummer Night's Dream* (I.i.13).

COMMON:

Such a playful rascal.

TRANSFORMED:

Such a merry, nimble, stirring spirit.

~ *Love's Labor's Lost* (V.ii.16).

and

The nimble-footed madcap Prince.

~ *Henry IV, Part One* (IV.i.95).

COMMON:

To have a really great time.

TRANSFORMED:

To make the coming hour o'erflow with joy, And pleasure down the brim.

~ *All's Well That Ends Well* (II.iv.46-47).

Enjoying Nature

EVEN YOUR MOTHER WOULD GROAN:
Mother nature is a great healer.

SO MAKE YOUR MAMA PROUD:

O, mickle is the powerful grace that lies
In plants, herbs, stones, and their true qualities.
~ *Romeo and Juliet* (II.iii.15-16).

You and your friends have had a wonderful weekend hiking in the woods. On the back of one of the gorgeous pictures you took of the adventure, you inscribe the above quote, taking care to change "mickle" to "lavish" or "wondrous," because no one but a shameless know-it-all has any chance of knowing the meaning of the word mickle.

OTHER COUPLETS – *Nature's Beauty Requires It*

COMMON:
What a beautiful sunrise.

TRANSFORMED:

Night's candles are burnt out, and jocund day
Stands tiptoe on the misty mountain tops.
~ *Romeo and Juliet* (III.v.9-10).

and

The morn in russet mantle clad
Walks o'er the dew of yon high eastward hill.
~ *Hamlet* (I.i.166).

COMMON:

What a gorgeous day.

TRANSFORMED:

**To solemnize this day the glorious sun
Stays in his course, and plays the alchemist,
Turning with the splendor of his precious eye
The meager cloddy earth to glittering gold.**

~ *King John* (III.i.77-80).

COMMON:

What a lovely sunset.

TRANSFORMED:

The sun begins to gild the western sky.

~ *The Two Gentlemen of Verona* (V.i.1).

COMMON:

What a wonderful world.

TRANSFORMED:

**O wonder!
How many goodly creatures are there here!
How beauteous mankind is! O brave new world
That has such people in it!**

~ *The Tempest* (V.i.182-184).

CHAPTER 6. DAILY THEATRICS –
All The World's A Stage

Let's face it – life affords so many opportunities for the grand gesture, the dramatic flair; but you do need the right material. Well now you have it. So prepare for your Shakespearean theatrical debut, as you seize the limelight with a display of verbal dexterity that will make you the envy of all your friends.

Bemoaning One's Fate

AVOID THE TEDIOUS:

Life's a drag!

AND CONVINCINGLY SIGH:

How weary, stale, flat and unprofitable
Seem to me all the uses of this world!

~ *Hamlet* (I.ii.133-134).

You're really down in the dumps, and the world seems to weigh heavily on your shoulders. The Bard has the perfect description for how you feel. Of course, you'll still feel rotten, but your consolation will be that now you'll sound magnificent in your misery!

Other Couplets –
So You Can Lament To Your Heart's Content

COMMON:

It's all so boring.

TRANSFORMED:

Tomorrow, and tomorrow, and tomorrow
Creeps in this petty pace from day to day,
To the last syllable of recorded time.
~ *Macbeth* (V.v.19-21).

COMMON:

I've lost everything but my agony.

TRANSFORMED:

You may my glories and my state depose,
But not my griefs; still am I king of those.
~ *Richard II* (IV.i.192-193).

COMMON:

My life is in the pits.

TRANSFORMED:

I am sworn brother... To grim Necessity, and he and I
Will keep a league till death.
~ *Richard II* (V.i.20-22).

COMMON:

I'm feeling really down.

TRANSFORMED:

Within me grief hath kept a tedious fast.
~ *Richard II* (II.i.75).

COMMON:

My life has been a disaster.

TRANSFORMED:

You see me here, you gods, a poor old man,
As full of grief as age, wretched in both.

~ *King Lear* (II.iv.272-273).

COMMON:

What's the point of it all?

TRANSFORMED:

Out, out, brief candle!
Life's but a walking shadow, a poor player
That struts and frets his hour upon the stage
And then is heard no more. It is a tale
Told by an idiot, full of sound and fury,
Signifying nothing.

~ *Macbeth* (V.v.23-28).

COMMON:

I've lost all hope.

TRANSFORMED:

I will despair, and be at enmity
With cozening Hope.

~ *Richard II* (II.ii.68-69).

[Note: Cozening = deceitful]

COMMON:

I've lost control of my life.

TRANSFORMED:

I am a feather for each wind that blows.

~ *The Winter's Tale* (II.iii.154).

COMMON:

I will sink like a stone.

TRANSFORMED:

I have a kind of alacrity in sinking.

~ *The Merry Wives of Windsor* (III.v.12-13).

Bemoaning A Mutual Fate

BRUSQUELY BLURT OUT:

Our goose is cooked.

OR SMOOTHLY ASSERT:

Come, we have no friend
But resolution and the briefest end.

~ *Antony and Cleopatra* (IV.xv.90-91).

Your neighborhood volleyball competition has a fearsome reputation, and you need to buck up your team's spirits. Your strategy calls for a mock-serious rendition of the above quote, as you enter the field of battle with a pronounced bounce in your step. Of course, if your teammates really do believe they have no chance, you have just sealed their doom. By that time, however, you will have already enjoyed the thrill of a grand Shakespearean entrance!

OTHER COUPLETS – *For The Woeful But Classy You*

COMMON:

We might as well give up all hope.

TRANSFORMED:

Comfort's in heaven, and we are on the earth,
Where nothing lives but crosses, cares, and griefs.
~ *Richard II* (II.ii.78-79).

COMMON:

Let's sit down and wail about our fate.

TRANSFORMED:

Will you sit down with me? and we two will rail
against our mistress the world, and all our misery.
~ *As You Like It* (III.ii.277-279).

COMMON:

God could care less about us.

TRANSFORMED:

As flies to wanton boys are we to the gods,
They kill us for their sport.
~ *King Lear* (IV.i.36-37).

COMMON:

Let's cry our eyes out!

TRANSFORMED:

Come weep with me – past hope, past cure, past help!
~ *Romeo and Juliet* (IV.i.45).

Risk Taking

TRITELY TAKE A BIG RISK:

This move could get me in trouble.

OR TAKE A CHANCE WITH STYLE:

In the boldness of my cunning, I will lay myself in hazard.

~ *Measure for Measure* (IV.ii.155-156).

You are taking quite a risk, and it's high time people recognized it. So, employing the above quote with no small amount of fanfare, you make precisely that point to everyone within earshot. Then again, the fact that they are all running for cover, even as you speak, might be telling you something you need to hear about the wisdom of your self-proclaimed boldness. In which case, you may want to switch your perspective, keep your mouth shut, and hightail it out of harm's way.

OTHER COUPLETS – *Because You Love A Challenge*

COMMON:

I'm looking for trouble.

TRANSFORMED:

My thoughts are ripe in mischief.

~ *Twelfth Night* (V.i.129).

COMMON:

I'm risking it all.

TRANSFORMED:

**I have set my life upon a cast,
And I will stand the hazard of the die.**

~ *Richard III* (V.iv.9-10).

Preparing To Trounce The Opposition

DON'T EMBARRASS YOURSELF:

I'll get my revenge.

SEIZE THE PRETENTIOUS MOMENT:

O, that the slave had forty thousand lives!
One is too poor, too weak for my revenge.

~ *Othello* (III.iii.442-443).

As the unchallenged sports expert at Oscar's Bar and Grill, you are shocked to find yourself babbling incoherently. It's all due to that stranger sitting on the bar stool next to you. She has had the sheer gall to challenge your longstanding baseball analysis with a dazzling array of fresh and pertinent facts. What an outrage! As she makes her disdainful exit from the bar, your brilliant "I'll show you" already has the crowd buzzing. And then you follow it up with a stirring rendition of the above quote, replacing, of course, "the slave" with "she." What a devastating counterpunch! Rest assured that everyone at Oscar's will draw the appropriate conclusion.

OTHER COUPLETS – *Time To Confront*

COMMON:

Revenge will be sweet.

TRANSFORMED:

The villainy you teach me, I will execute, and it shall
go hard but I will better the instruction.

~ *The Merchant of Venice* (III.i.71-73).

COMMON:

There's a time for peace and a time for war.

TRANSFORMED:

In peace there's nothing so becomes a man
As modest stillness and humility;
But when the blast of war blows in our ears,
Then imitate the action of the tiger.

~ *Henry V* (III.i.3-6).

COMMON:

I'll expose these hypocrites.

TRANSFORMED:

Now step I forth to whip hypocrisy.

~ *Love's Labor's Lost* (IV.iii.149).

Sucking It Up

THEY MAY DOUBT WHAT YOU SAY:

It doesn't hurt a bit.

BUT BE IMPRESSED WITH HOW YOU SAY IT:

[These are] scars to move laughter only.

~ *Coriolanus* (III.iii.52).

It doesn't matter whether the wound is physical or psychological –you're not going to let it get you down. So, when someone asks about it, you know exactly what to quote. And you will do it with that little half-laugh you have so beautifully mastered over the years. Absolutely no one will suggest that you're kidding yourself.

OTHER COUPLETS –
Because You Are One Tough Customer

COMMON:

I'm as macho as any man.

TRANSFORMED:

I dare do all that may become a man;
Who dares do more is none.

~ *Macbeth* (I.vii.46-47).

COMMON:

Stop quaking and get a grip.

TRANSFORMED:

We fail?
But screw your courage to the sticking place,
And we'll not fail.

~ *Macbeth* (I.vii.59-61).

Going Into Battle

IT'S SO BANAL TO SAY:

Let's get it on!

SO CATCH THEM OFF GUARD:

Lay on, Macduff,
And damned be him that first cries, "Hold, enough!"

~ *Macbeth* (V.viii.33-34).

Whatever the impending battle – bridge, golf, tennis – you've got the brave words you need to engage your own Macduff, for example, Bob, Nate or Cindy. Of course, when Macbeth said these words to his enemy, he didn't exactly triumph. But then you didn't kill a king and gratuitously insult some nasty witches.

OTHER COUPLETS – *Because You're Ready For Combat*

COMMON:
Let the battle begin!
TRANSFORMED:
Cry "Havoc!" and let slip the dogs of war.
~ *Julius Caesar* (III.i.273).

COMMON:
Charge!
TRANSFORMED:
Once more unto the breach, dear friends, once more.
~ *Henry V* (III.i.1).

COMMON:
The soldier has returned to the battle.
TRANSFORMED:
Mars's hot minion is return'd again.
~ *The Tempest* (IV.i.98).

Displaying Courage

TRUE BUT PARDON OUR YAWNS:
Don't let fear of death rob you of the courage to live.
NOW YOUR COURAGE SPEAKS VOLUMES:
Cowards die many times before their deaths,
The valiant never taste of death but once.
~ *Julius Caesar* (II.ii.32-33).

It was good enough for Caesar and it's good enough for you. As you prepare yourself for the battle to come you feel a surge of courage and resolve. Your teammates, by the process of moral osmosis, are imbued with the same sense of confidence and fortitude. Your quote is just what they need as they charge onto the bocce ball court!

OTHER COUPLETS –
Courage Is Your Middle Name

COMMON:

Everyone knows I am as tough as nails.

TRANSFORMED:

Danger knows full well
That Caesar is more dangerous than he.

~ *Julius Caesar* (II.ii.44-45).

[Note: Change "Caesar" to the name of your person of choice.]

COMMON:

Time to fight.

TRANSFORMED:

This is no world
To play with mammets and to tilt with lips.
We must have bloody noses and cracked crowns.

~ *Henry IV, Part One* (II.iii.91-93).

[Note: Mammets = dolls]

Exchanging Barbs

BELIE YOUR WORDS:

Don't try to match wits with me.

OR PROVE YOUR POINT:

**If you spend word for word with me, I shall
make your wit bankrupt.**

~ *The Two Gentlemen of Verona* (II.iv.41-42).

You are watching an ill-advised attempt by a very inexperienced fellow to take on the most fearsome member of your group, a woman so skilled with the verbal rapier that the only fortunate thing about her thrusts is that they cause an immediate, rather than a lingering, demise. You take him aside and get to the point: "If you spend word for word with her, she will make your wit bankrupt. Withdraw now while you have a chance."

OTHER COUPLETS –
Verbal Fisticuffs On Display

COMMON:

Her sharp tongue is hard to take!

TRANSFORMED:

**O God, sir, here's a dish I love not,
I cannot endure my Lady Tongue.**

~ *Much Ado About Nothing* (II.i.274-275).

COMMON:

They're always going at each other.

TRANSFORMED:

They never meet but there's a skirmish of wit between them.

~ *Much Ado About Nothing* (I.i.63-64).

Stepping Up To The Plate

YOU KNOW YOU MUST SAY IT:

Don't blow your big chance.

SO SAY IT WITH A FLOURISH:

There is a tide in the affairs of men,
Which taken at the flood, leads on to fortune;
Omitted, all the voyage of their life
Is bound in shallows and in miseries.
On such a full sea are we now afloat,
And we must take the current when it serves,
Or lose our ventures.

~ *Julius Caesar* (IV.iii.218-223).

The message is a simple one: "When opportunity knocks, don't be a fool; open the door. You may never get another chance." The quote is a bit long, but it's perfect for an e-mail or card to a friend who needs to find the courage to make a big decision.

Other Couplets – *Let's Get Cracking*

COMMON:

Get on with it!

TRANSFORMED:

**If it were done, when 'tis done, then 'twere well
It were done quickly.**

~ *Macbeth* (I.vii.1-2).

COMMON:

You can count on me.

TRANSFORMED:

**I will not be slack
To play my part in Fortune's pageant.**

~ *Henry VI, Part Two* (I.ii.66-67).

Hamming It Up

YOU DO SOUND PITIFUL:

Has anyone ever been so abused?

SO PLAY IT TO THE HILT:

**O... she hath tied
Sharp-toothed unkindness, like a vulture, here.**

~ *King Lear* (II.iv.134-135).

This quote is ideal for the melodrama you're aching to create as, gender adjusting if necessary, you bemoan the inconsiderate behavior of another. Be sure to have an audience for this one as, pointing to your heart, you crescendo to "like a vulture, here."

OTHER COUPLETS –
So You Can Continue To Serve The Ham

COMMON:

It's a disgrace.

TRANSFORMED:

Such an act
That blurs the grace and blush of modesty.
~ *Hamlet* (III.iv.40-41).

COMMON:

I'm going to speak my mind, no matter what.

TRANSFORMED:

I'll speak… though hell itself should gape
And bid me hold my peace.
~ *Hamlet* (I.ii.244-245).

Really Hamming It Up

SPEAK IN A LOW, PATHETIC VOICE:

Nothing's as bad as the ingratitude of others.

OR PUMP UP THE VOLUME:

Blow, blow, thou winter wind,
Thou art not so unkind
As man's ingratitude.
~ *As You Like It* (II.vii.174-176).

This is even hammier than the vulture quote and there is an element of risk in surrendering to its charms. The hazard lies in the potential for others to brazenly suggest that "blow, blow thou winter wind" has altogether too much in common with your recently acquired Shakespearean erudition. It's absurd, of course, but one must be prepared for the rampant envy that is sure to accompany your growing brilliance.

OTHER COUPLETS – *High Drama Indeed*

COMMON:

There's no excuse for this ungrateful behavior.

TRANSFORMED:

Run to your houses, fall upon your knees,
Pray to the gods to intermit the plague
That needs must light on this ingratitude.
~ *Julius Caesar* (I.i.53-55).

COMMON:

Cold-hearted thanklessness.

TRANSFORMED:

Ingratitude! thou marble-hearted fiend.
~ *King Lear* (I.iv.259).

Rising To The Pomposity Occasion

OVERBLOWN:

Oh, I am a magnificent wreck!

WONDERFULLY BUMPTIOUS:

Down, down I come, like glist'ring Phaeton,
Wanting the manage of unruly jades...
Down court! down king!
For night-owls shriek where mounting larks
should sing.
~ *Richard II* (III.iii.178-183).

These are the words of King Richard II as he reacts to his throne being usurped. He is determined to meet his fate with a flourish. You can do the same, of course, but hopefully for something infinitely less tragic. For example, you may have been invited to dinner at the home of your husband's parents, and you are dreading it like the plague. You dutifully dress up for the occasion but, as you descend the stairs from your bedroom, you can't resist quoting these delectably self-pitying words, changing "court" to "wife" and "king" to "queen." If you stop at "unruly jades" (which means uncontrollable horses) you will have tasted the sweet nectar, but the full quote will make for a delicious drink indeed.

OTHER COUPLETS – *By All Means, Overdo It*

COMMON:

This is what I get for telling the truth.

TRANSFORMED:

Take note, take note, O world,
To be direct and honest is not safe.
~ *Othello* (III.iii.377-378).

COMMON:

What a wretched creature I am!

TRANSFORMED:

O, what a rogue and peasant slave am I!
~ *Hamlet* (II.ii.550).

COMMON:

On your knees, now!

TRANSFORMED:

We are amazed, and thus long have we stood
To watch the fearful bending of thy knee.

~ *Richard II* (III.iii.72-73).

Reckoning With Fortune

PITEOUSLY DOWNCAST:

I'm just fulfilling my role, no matter how sad.

WOEFUL BUT CLASSY:

I hold the world but as the world …
A stage, where every man must play his part,
And mine a sad one.

~ *The Merchant of Venice* (I.i.77-79).

Dame Fortune has once again abandoned you at the last moment, and you find yourself on the losing end of a contest that would have been so sweet to win. When your sympathetic friend offers condolences, you respond with the above quote, taking care to look truly pitiful while you say it.

OTHER COUPLETS – *In The Hands Of Fate*

COMMON:

Destiny's darling.

TRANSFORMED:

Sweet Fortune's minion and her pride.

~ *Henry IV, Part One* (I.i.83).

COMMON:

You're both lucky and good.

TRANSFORMED:

Nature and Fortune joined to make thee great.

~ *King John* (III.i.52).

COMMON:

We all have our roles to play in life.

TRANSFORMED:

All the world's a stage,

And all the men and women merely players.

~ *As You Like It* (II.vii.139-140).

Putting Reputation On Trial

CHOOSE YET ANOTHER TIRED PROTESTATION:

My reputation is everything to me.

OR GET THE RESPECT YOU DESERVE:

The purest treasure mortal times afford

Is spotless reputation; that away,

Men are but gilded loam or painted clay.

~ *Richard II* (I.i.177-179).

At the local Starbucks you are being roundly condemned by a number of your friends for your penny-pinching ways. Adopting a "deeply hurt" look, you wade in with the above gem from the Bard. But the situation goes painfully awry when your gorgeous new girlfriend walks into the coffee shop and inquires as to the occasion for your Shakespearean erudition. Before your friends make the inconvenient mistake of loudly proclaiming your tightwad tendencies, you chime in with a veritable ode to the virtues of generosity, lest one become mere "gilded loam or painted clay." Quite pleasantly satisfied, your new sweetie quickly snuggles in next to you and orders a vanilla latte. Not being a complete idiot, you pick up the tab.

OTHER COUPLETS – *It's All About Respect*

COMMON:

Don't mess with my reputation.

TRANSFORMED:

Who steals my purse steals trash;
'tis something, nothing;
'Twas mine, 'tis his, and has been slave to thousands;
But he who filches from me my good name
Robs me of that which not enriches him,
And makes me poor indeed.
~ *Othello* (III.iii.157-161).

COMMON:

They trashed my character.

TRANSFORMED:

Reputation, reputation, reputation! O, I have lost my
reputation! I have lost the immortal part of myself,
and what remains is bestial.
~ *Othello* (II.iii.262-264).

COMMON:

Falsely accused.

TRANSFORMED:

Pierced to the soul with slander's venomed spear.
~ *Richard II* (I.i.171).

COMMON:

Not even the powerful can stop tongues from wagging.

TRANSFORMED:

What king so strong
Can tie the gall up in the slanderous tongue?

~ *Measure for Measure* (III.ii.187-188).

Staying Above The Crowd

SPARE US:

I'm above such things.

AND BEGUILE WITH:

You are idle shallow things; I am not of your element.

~ *Twelfth Night* (III.iv.123-124).

The party is getting louder and more unrestrained by the minute. But you are focusing your energies on the much more refined activity of contemplating the physical charms of that lovely/handsome vision across the room. When the revelers ask you to join them, you give them a dismissive wave of the hand and disdainfully give voice to the above quote. The fact that you can say this while continuing to indulge in erotic contemplation only serves to demonstrate the remarkable verbal dexterity you have achieved thanks to this book. It does not indicate shameless hypocrisy.

OTHER COUPLETS – *So You Can Really Feel Superior*

COMMON:
Temptation is no temptation to me.

TRANSFORMED:
The unstooping firmness of my upright soul.
~ *Richard II* (I.i.121).

COMMON:
He's the farthest thing from lazy.

TRANSFORMED:
Not sleeping, to engross his idle body,
But praying, to enrich his watchful soul.
~ *Richard III* (III.vii.76-77).

Maneuvering Deviously

MOVE NO ONE:
He knew how to work a crowd.

OR MOVE QUITE A FEW:
How he did seem to dive into their hearts
With humble and familiar courtesy.
~ *Richard II* (I.iv.25-26).

He is a sickening, unctuous toady but he thinks he's so clever. And just because everyone has fallen for his oily charms doesn't mean you can't cut him down to size with a withering quote. So when one of his newly anointed devotees is waxing wonderful about him, feel free to employ the above gem, culminating in these prescient words: "But he will be shown to be a snake soon enough."

OTHER COUPLETS – *What A Wily Rascal*

COMMON:

They can be led around by the nose.

TRANSFORMED:

They'll take suggestion as a cat laps milk.

~ *The Tempest* (II.i.288).

COMMON:

I love it when a plan comes together.

TRANSFORMED:

Now does my project gather to a head.

~ *The Tempest* (V.i.1).

COMMON:

Let's pull the wool over her eyes.

TRANSFORMED:

Then go we near her, that her ear lose nothing
Of the false sweet bait that we lay for it.

~ *Much Ado About Nothing* (III.i.32-33).

COMMON:

Pretend to be sweet and innocent.

TRANSFORMED:

Look like the innocent flower,
But be the serpent under it.

~ *Macbeth* (I.v.66).

CHAPTER 7. Seriously Now –
The Abundant Dolor Of The Heart

As we all know, there are moments when life takes on a somber tone. Be assured that Shakespeare, with dignity and sensitivity, can deliver the desired poignancy.

A Brief And Elegant Eulogy

THE COMPLIMENT PROSAIC:
He lived a beautiful life.

THE COMPLIMENT SUBLIME:
His life was gentle, and the elements
So mix'd in him that Nature might stand up
And say to all the world, "This was a man!"
~ *Julius Caesar* (V.v.73-75).

To Shakespeare there could be no greater compliment than simply to say, "This was a man." Of course, our more enlightened era would insist that "This was a woman" is equally laudable. I love this quote and, with gender adjustment, know exactly when and how I hope to use it. Perhaps, you do too.

Other Couplets – *This Person Is Special*

COMMON:

He was truly one of a kind.

TRANSFORMED:

[He]was a man, take him for all in all,
I shall not look upon his like again.

~ *Hamlet* (I.ii.187-188).

COMMON:

He lived a resolute life.

TRANSFORMED:

Fare thee well, great heart! …
This earth that bears thee dead
Bears not alive so stout a gentleman.

~ *Henry IV, Part One* (V.iv.87-93).

COMMON:

Some things are worth dying for.

TRANSFORMED:

He lives in fame that died in virtue's cause.

~ *Titus Andronicus* (I.i.390).

COMMON:

He died well.

TRANSFORMED:

Nothing in his life
Became him like the leaving it.

~ *Macbeth* (I.iv.7-8).

In Touch With Grief

YOUR GRIEF DESERVES BETTER:
I'll never get over this.

INFINITELY BETTER:

My particular grief
Is of so flood-gate and o'erbearing nature
That it engluts and swallows other sorrows,
And it is still itself.
~ *Othello* (I.iii.55-58).

These words have to be reserved for a sorrow or tragedy that is overwhelming, such as the death of a parent, spouse or child. At such times no words will ever be adequate, but at least this quote has the virtue of embracing the grief rather than suppressing it.

OTHER COUPLETS – *This Sorrow Is Profound*

COMMON:
He/she is utterly heartbroken.

TRANSFORMED:

A heart
As full of sorrows as the sea of sands.
~ *The Two Gentlemen of Verona* (IV.iii.32-33).

COMMON:
I'm much more miserable than I look.

TRANSFORMED:

I have that within which passes show,
These but the trappings and the suits of woe.
~ *Hamlet* (I.ii.85-86).

COMMON:

This will be my final resting place.

TRANSFORMED:

O, here
Will I set up my everlasting rest,
And shake the yoke of inauspicious stars
From this world-wearied flesh.

~ *Romeo and Juliet* (V.iii.109-112).

COMMON:

It will take some time to get used to this ordeal.

TRANSFORMED:

Give sorrow leave a while to tutor me
To this submission.

~ *Richard II* (IV.i.166-167).

Unspeakable Anguish

NO WORDS CAN REALLY CAPTURE IT:

I can't bear the fact that I'll never see you again.

THESE COME CLOSE:

Why should a dog, a horse, a rat, have life,
And thou no breath at all? Thou'lt come no more,
Never, never, never, never, never!

~ *King Lear* (V.iii.307-309).

It has been said that there are no more poignant words in all of Shakespeare than these words spoken by Lear on the death of his daughter Cordelia. What could be a more direct arrow to the heart than these five "nevers" when reflecting on the death of a loved one. To amend Voltaire a bit, after such heart-wrenching redundancy, if there weren't an afterlife, it would be necessary to invent one.

OTHER COUPLETS – *Such Heartache*

COMMON:

There's nothing left worth bothering about.

TRANSFORMED:

**All is but toys: renown and grace is dead,
The wine of life is drawn, and the mere lees
Is left this vault to brag of.**

~ *Macbeth* (II.iii.94-96).

COMMON:

Leave him alone – he's suffered enough.

TRANSFORMED:

**He hates him
That would upon the rack of this tough world
Stretch him out longer.**

~ *King Lear* (V.iii.314-316).

COMMON:

A great mind now ravaged by disease.

TRANSFORMED:

O, what a noble mind is here o'erthrown!

~ *Hamlet* (III.i.150).

Expressing Sorrow

MOURNFUL:
I'll miss him till the day I die.

SOUL-STIRRING:
I honored him, I loved him, and I will weep
My date of life out for his sweet life's loss.
~ *King John* (IV.iii.106).

This poignant quote belongs on a card that acknowledges the passing of a loved one, with appropriate gender adjustment. Some may find it a bit melodramatic; but, for many others, it will capture the feeling of inconsolable sorrow that one can have at such a time.

OTHER COUPLETS – *So Much Sadness*

COMMON:
I'll keep my grief to myself.

TRANSFORMED:
Friends, I owe more tears
To this dead man than you shall see me pay.
~ *Julius Caesar* (V.iii.101-102).

COMMON:
This tragedy has me at a loss for words.

TRANSFORMED:
I have too few [words]
... When the tongue's office should be prodigal
To breathe the abundant dolor of the heart.
~ *Richard II* (I.iii.255-257).

Coping With Life's Trials

AN EXCELLENT SENTIMENT AND A GOOD CHOICE OF WORDS:

Grace under pressure.

AN EXCELLENT SENTIMENT AND A MARVELOUS CHOICE OF WORDS:

Happy is your Grace
That can translate the stubbornness of fortune
Into so quiet and so sweet a style.

~ *As You Like It* (II.i.18-20).

There are people in this world who endure incredible challenges with such grace and dignity that you absolutely must acknowledge them. Fortunately, for that special moment, we have this truly wonderful quote.

OTHER COUPLETS – *Dealing With Adversity*

COMMON:

If I have to die, I'll die with dignity.

TRANSFORMED:

If I must die,
I will encounter darkness as a bride,
And hug it in mine arms.

~ *Measure for Measure* (III.i.82-84).

COMMON:

With light hearts we charge into this hopeless battle.

TRANSFORMED:

Doomsday is near, die all, die merrily.

~ *Henry IV, Part One* (IV.i.134).

COMMON:

You've got to get on with your life.

TRANSFORMED:

Moderate lamentation is the right of the dead,
Excessive grief the enemy to the living.

~ *All's Well That Ends Well* (I.i.55-56).

COMMON:

There are a lot of people worse off than we are.

TRANSFORMED:

This wide and universal theatre
Presents more woeful pageants than the scene
Wherein we play.

~ *As You Like It* (II.vii.137-139).

COMMON:

You can't take it with you.

TRANSFORMED:

And nothing can we call our own but death,
And that small model of the barren earth
Which serves as paste and cover to our bones.

~ *Richard II* (III.ii.152-154).

COMMON:

Don't cry over what you can't change.

TRANSFORMED:

What's gone and what's past help,
Should be past grief.

~ *The Winter's Tale* (III.ii.222-223).

Willing To Pay The Price

NOBILITY DESERVES BETTER:

What amazing self-sacrifice.

THIS IS BETTER:

Upon such sacrifices…
The gods themselves throw incense.

~ *King Lear* (V.iii.20-21).

Your friend has just sacrificed everything for the noblest of purposes. Why not send a card to him or her with words like these: "Your courageous action speaks volumes for your character and I am incredibly proud of you. Upon such sacrifices, my dear friend, the gods themselves throw incense." Given the consequences of such noble action, however, you may privately thank the same divinity for not tapping your shoulder for the assignment.

OTHER COUPLETS – *Staying Steadfast*

COMMON:

Don't give in, no matter what.

TRANSFORMED:

Yield not thy neck
To fortune's yoke, but let thy dauntless mind
Still ride in triumph over all mischance.

~ *Henry VI, Part Three* (III.iii.16-18).

COMMON:

You won't find me being a crybaby.

TRANSFORMED:

I will instruct my sorrows to be proud.

~ *King John* (III.i.68).

A Beautiful Goodbye

TOUCHING BUT STALE:

May he rest in peace.

BEYOND TOUCHING:

Now cracks a noble heart. Good night, sweet prince,
And flights of angels sing thee to thy rest!

~ *Hamlet* (V.ii.359-360).

I used this quote on the occasion of the death of one of the sweetest people I have ever known – my Aunt Mae. My wife and I had been visiting her at the hospital where she was dying of cancer. On one occasion, shortly before her death, she said to us that she wished her soul could just sprout wings, escape her agonized body, and float to heaven. A few weeks later at the funeral parlor, I was asked to sign the register. As I did so, the above words from Hamlet leapt into my mind and I wrote, "Goodbye, sweet Mae, and flights of angels sing thee to thy rest." Others who read it were quite moved because, for all of us, it was easy to envision that such a lovely soul deserved an angelic escort.

OTHER COUPLETS – *It Needs To Be Said Well*

COMMON:

Even the young get old and die.

TRANSFORMED:

Fear no more the heat o' th' sun,
Nor the furious winter's rages,
Thou thy worldly task hast done,
Home art gone, and ta'en thy wages.
Golden lads and girls all must,
As chimney-sweepers, come to dust.

~ *Cymbeline* (IV.ii.258-263).

COMMON:

He looks so peaceful now.

TRANSFORMED:

After life's fitful fever he sleeps well.

~ *Macbeth* (III.ii.23).

CHAPTER 8. WISE COUNSEL –
We'll Teach You To Drink Deep

The competition to be the wise counselor of the group can be pretty stiff at times. But you, alone among your peers, have the Elizabethan master to give your commentary an added depth and impact. A reputation for sagacity is only a few quotes away.

In Times Of Adversity

POINT MADE, BUT NOT WELL-MADE:
You're doing fine but I'm still in hell.

WELL-MADE, INDEED:

Thou art a soul in bliss, but I am bound
Upon a wheel of fire, that mine own tears
Do scald like molten lead.

~ *King Lear* (IV.vii.45-47).

Two friends at a point in time – the one newly married, happily employed, on top of the world; the other, just divorced, between jobs, and thoroughly miserable. When the former complains to you about the latter's constant whining, you respond: "Don't forget that she has experienced a series of devastating events this past year. As Shakespeare said, 'You are a soul in bliss, but she is bound upon a wheel of fire that her own tears do scald like molten lead.'"

Other Couplets – *They Are So Distraught*

COMMON:

There is so much suffering in life.

TRANSFORMED:

**Each new morn
New widows howl, new orphans cry, new sorrows
Strike heaven on the face.**

~ *Macbeth* (IV.iii.4-6).

COMMON:

What a foolish world we live in.

TRANSFORMED:

**When we are born, we cry that we are come
To this great stage of fools.**

~ *King Lear* (IV.vi.182-183).

COMMON:

I'm in no mood to be nice.

TRANSFORMED:

**The thorny point
Of bare distress hath taken from me the show
Of smooth civility.**

~ *As You Like It* (II.vii.94-96).

All In Due Time

GIVE THEM BANALITY:

For everything there is a season.

OR GIVE PROFUNDITY A VOICE:

Men must endure
Their going hence even as their coming hither,
Ripeness is all.

~ *King Lear* (V.ii.9-11).

You've won the trophy as the best tennis player in your group for the past three years. But this year your legs have lost a little too much of their spring – and you succumb to younger competition. At the awards dinner you show the kind of class that would make your family proud and say, "I'm grateful for my past awards but now it's time for a changing of the guard." And then you quote the Bard like the true winner you are, gender adjusting to taste.

OTHER COUPLETS – *Time Doesn't Stand Still*

COMMON:

Nothing is at its peak for long.

TRANSFORMED:

Every thing that grows
Holds in perfection but a little moment.

~ *Sonnet 15* (1-2).

COMMON:
Decay will inevitably happen.

TRANSFORMED:
And so from hour to hour, we ripe and ripe,
And then, from hour to hour, we rot and rot;
And thereby hangs a tale.
~ *As You Like It* (II.vii.26-28).

Heavenly Intervention

YOU MAY BE RIGHT:
Everything happens for a purpose.

SO SAY IT WITH STYLE:
There is special providence in the fall of a sparrow.
~ *Hamlet* (V.ii.219-220).

This is the perfect quote if you want to insist that nothing happens by chance in a world lovingly guided by Providence. A bit too apple-pie for some folks perhaps, but some of your counselees may derive enormous comfort from this optimistic sentiment. Besides, on those rare occasions when your counseling techniques fall flat (hard to believe, I know), what better way to soothe a dejected client than to suggest that a power even greater than your skill will make all things right in the end. Yes, even the Bard can benefit from the Ultimate Backup.

OTHER COUPLETS – *The Celestial Powers Are At Work*

COMMON:

We don't always know what's good for us.

TRANSFORMED:

**We, ignorant of ourselves,
Beg often our own harms, which the wise powers
Deny us for our good; so find we profit
By losing of our prayers.**
~ *Antony and Cleopatra* (II.i.5-8).

COMMON:

God help us!

TRANSFORMED:

Angels and ministers of grace defend us!
~ *Hamlet* (I.iv.39).

COMMON:

You're in touch with the divine.

TRANSFORMED:

Methinks in thee some blessed spirit doth speak.
~ *All's Well That Ends Well* (II.i.175).

COMMON:

God's will prevails.

TRANSFORMED:

**There's a divinity that shapes our ends,
Rough-hew them how we will.**
~ *Hamlet* (V.ii.10-11).

and

What can be avoided
Whose end is purposed by the mighty gods?
~ *Julius Caesar* (II.ii.26-27).

COMMON:
God's will be done.

TRANSFORMED:
Heaven hath a hand in these events,
To whose high will we bound our calm contents.
~ *Richard II* (V.ii.37-38).

Probing Life's Mysteries

THIRST INDUCING:
Time for some soul searching.

THIRST QUENCHING:
We'll teach you to drink deep ere you depart.
~ *Hamlet* (I.ii.175).

Your counselees may be desperate for answers to their concerns, but you are wise enough to know that some problems don't come with easy answers. Besides you may not have a clue as to what to say. Face it, you need an opener that will simultaneously instill confidence, impress your counselee, and buy you some time. The above quote fits the bill perfectly. It's true that promising to "drink deep" could be raising expectations too high, but the path to Shakespearean counselor greatness is not for the faint of heart.

OTHER COUPLETS – *It's Time To Go Deep*

COMMON:

Time to face the truth.

TRANSFORMED:

You shall not budge ... till I set you up a glass
Where you may see the inmost part of you.

~ *Hamlet* (III.iv.18-20).

COMMON:

To reflect what reality is.

TRANSFORMED:

To hold as 'twere the mirror up to nature.

~ *Hamlet* (III.ii.22).

COMMON:

I'm going to make you feel it in your gut.

TRANSFORMED:

Peace, sit you down,
And let me wring your heart.

~ *Hamlet* (III.iv.34-35).

COMMON:

He strove mightily for self-knowledge.

TRANSFORMED:

One that, above all other strifes, contended
especially to know himself.

~ *Measure for Measure* (III.ii.232-233).

Everything In Moderation

EXCESSIVELY USED:

Don't overdo it.

USED EVER SO RARELY:

They are as sick that surfeit with too much as they that starve with nothing.

~ *The Merchant of Venice* (I.ii.5-7).

This is a genteel way of telling someone not to overdo it. So genteel, perhaps, that the recipient of your cleverness may not have a clue as to what you are saying. Fortunately, you have become far too savvy to be thwarted by the small matter of recipient bewilderment. That is why you smoothly add this clarification: "In other words, don't overdo it."

OTHER COUPLETS – *Keeping Everything In A Low Key*

COMMON:

With us, only a soft approach will work.

TRANSFORMED:

Your gentleness shall force,
More than your force move us to gentleness.

~ *As You Like It* (II.vii.102-103).

COMMON:

Take it slowly and think it out carefully.

TRANSFORMED:

Let your own discretion be your tutor.

~ *Hamlet* (III.ii.16-17).

COMMON:

Let's be prudent about this.

TRANSFORMED:

Let's teach ourselves that honorable stop,
Not to outsport discretion.

~ *Othello* (II.iii.2-3).

COMMON:

You're only making things worse.

TRANSFORMED:

Fie, fie, fie!
This is the way to kindle, not to quench.

~ *Coriolanus* (III.i.195-196).

Whatever Will Be, Will Be

NOT GOOD ENOUGH:

Don't sweat what you can't change.

BETTER THAN GOOD:

Things past redress are now with me past care.

~ *Richard II* (II.iii.171).

Knowing when to worry about something and when to let it go is perhaps as close to true wisdom as one can achieve. Most of us have a long way to go to arrive at this hallowed state; but no matter how far we are from that admirable goal, we are never too far to resist "enlightening" others. Since the above quote is quite pithy, be prepared to follow up with a generous helping of your own material.

OTHER COUPLETS – *It Is What It Is*

COMMON:
Don't cry over spilt milk.

TRANSFORMED:
What's done cannot be undone.
~ *Macbeth* (V.i.68).

COMMON:
It both helps and hurts.

TRANSFORMED:
It makes him, and it mars him.
~ *Macbeth* (II.iii.32).

Hanging Tough

TRUE:
You can't let bad luck get you down.

BUT BETTER SAID:
**Of your philosophy you make no use,
If you give place to accidental evils.**
~ *Julius Caesar* (IV.iii.146).

You recreational vehicle has just blown a tire and left you and your traveling companions stranded on a mountain road. What a perfect time for you to instruct your little group on the importance of not getting in the dumps of despair. You're absolutely sure that the group needs your special brand of wisdom, so you ply them with the above quote. Funny thing – after prolonged exposure to your inspiring words, your traveling companions have now arrived at consensus regarding who is going to "volunteer" to walk five miles to the nearest town for help. To paraphrase the Bible, an even more revered source than the Bard, "A prophet is not without honor – except in his own Winnebago."

OTHER COUPLETS – *Rugged As Can Be*

COMMON:

When the going gets tough, the tough get going.

TRANSFORMED:

In the reproof of chance
Lies the true proof of men.

~ *Troilus and Cressida* (I.iii.33-34).

COMMON:

Accept what you can't avoid.

TRANSFORMED:

What cannot be eschewed must be embraced.

~ *The Merry Wives of Windsor* (V.v.237).

Human Frailty

NOT AN EASY SELL:

Their faults just make them more lovable.

BUT NOW YOU HAVE A CHANCE:

They say, best men are moulded out of faults,
And for the most, become much more the better
For being a little bad.

~ *Measure for Measure* (V.i.439-441).

This quote is a great comfort to those of us who, spiritually speaking, "still need work," as a friend of mine would say. It's nice to know that our faults make us all the more lovable. Naturally, we could eliminate them on the spot; but then we would be disappointing our loved ones, who love us because of our faults. It's a difficult concept to grasp, and only the truly enlightened can do so. For some reason, my beloved wife views my interpretation of this quote with withering disdain.

OTHER COUPLETS – *It's An Imperfect World*

COMMON:
The only blemish on his character.

TRANSFORMED:
The only soil of his fair virtue's gloss.
~ *Love's Labor's Lost* (II.i.47).

COMMON:
People in glass houses shouldn't throw stones.

TRANSFORMED:
Forbear to judge, for we are sinners all.
~ *Henry VI, Part Two* (III.iii.31).

COMMON:
Nothing stays perfect forever.

TRANSFORMED:
In the sweetest bud
The eating canker dwells.
~ *The Two Gentlemen of Verona* (I.i.42-43).

The Value Of Suffering

SHORT AND TEDIOUS:

No pain, no gain.

SHORT AND FASCINATING:

Lest too light winning
Make the prize light.

~ *The Tempest* (I.ii.452-453).

You need to buck up a friend who is starting to waver in his or her resolve to meet a very difficult challenge. This quote is perfect to make your point. Depending on your friend's mood, however, you may be gratefully praised for your wisdom or find yourself nursing a little pain of your own.

OTHER COUPLETS – *Finding The Positive*

COMMON:

Roses grow among thorns.

TRANSFORMED:

The strawberry grows underneath the nettle.

~ *Henry V* (I.i.60).

COMMON:

Not everyone will lose out.

TRANSFORMED:

Ill blows the wind that profits nobody.

~ *Henry VI, Part Three* (II.v.55).

COMMON:

Suffering leads to wisdom.

TRANSFORMED:

Adversity's sweet milk, philosophy.

~ *Romeo and Juliet* (III.iii.55).

Expectations Turned Upside Down

WISE BUT STALE:

If it ain't broke, don't fix it.

WISE AND FRESH:

Striving to better, oft we mar what's well.

~ *King Lear* (I.iv.346).

Good advice for those individuals who, despite good intentions, sometimes butt in when they shouldn't. This can't possibly apply to you, but I am itching to use this quote on a couple of good friends of mine who shall remain anonymous.

OTHER COUPLETS – *You Just Never Know*

COMMON:

Appearances can be deceiving.

TRANSFORMED:

Things sweet to taste prove in digestion sour.

~ *Richard II* (I.iii.236).

COMMON:

Virtue doesn't always pay, nor vice go unrewarded.

TRANSFORMED:

Some rise by sin, and some by virtue fall.

~ *Measure for Measure* (II.i.38).

COMMON:

Bad things happen to good people.

TRANSFORMED:

Some innocents scape not the thunderbolt.

~ *Antony and Cleopatra* (II.v. 77).

COMMON:

The necessary storm before the calm.

TRANSFORMED:

When Fortune means to men most good,
She looks upon them with a threatening eye.

~ *King John* (III.iv.120).

Patience Is A Virtue

WHAT'S TRITE:

Don't let it get to you.

AND WHAT'S NOT:

What cannot be preserved when Fortune takes,
Patience her injury a mockery makes.

~ *Othello* (I.iii.206-207).

Every wise counselor needs at least one "patience" quote in his or her repertoire, especially when it's connected with psychological wounds. This little beauty is not so long as to try the very virtue it extols.

OTHER COUPLETS – *Composure Is Your Middle Name*

COMMON:

Time heals all wounds.

TRANSFORMED:

How poor are they who have not patience!
What wound did ever heal but by degrees?
~ *Othello* (II.iii.370-371).

COMMON:

I could have endured anything but this.

TRANSFORMED:

Had it pleased heaven
To try me with affliction, had they rained
All kinds of sores and shames on my bare head...
I should have found in some place of my soul
A drop of patience... [but] to be discarded thence!
~ *Othello* (IV.ii.48-53).

COMMON:

Even the worst day eventually ends.

TRANSFORMED:

Come what come may,
Time and the hour runs through the roughest day.
~ *Macbeth* (I.iii.146-147).

COMMON:
Curiosity killed the cat.

TRANSFORMED:
Thus hath the candle singed the moth.
~ *The Merchant of Venice* (II.ix.79).

COMMON:
Calm yourself down.

TRANSFORMED:
Upon the heat and flame of thy distemper
Sprinkle cool patience!
~ *Hamlet* (III.iv.123-124).

COMMON:
Please God, don't let me lose my temper.

TRANSFORMED:
O you blessed ministers above,
Keep me in patience.
~ *Measure for Measure* (V.i.115-116).

Sage Advice

BE TERMINALLY INSIPID:
Physician heal thyself.

OR TAKE THE CURE:
For there was never yet philosopher
That could endure the toothache patiently.
~ *Much Ado About Nothing* (V.i.35-36).

Some people feel quite free to lecture others on how to deal with their pain. But, of course, they so often can't cope with their own pain. When such a person has just regaled you with his or her philosophical bromides, feel free to employ the above quote with all the righteousness you can muster.

OTHER COUPLETS – *Perspectives on Suffering*

COMMON:
It's easy to solve other people's problems.

TRANSFORMED:
Every one [can] master a grief but he that has it.
~ *Much Ado About Nothing* (III.ii.28-29).

COMMON:
Don't sugarcoat the pain.

TRANSFORMED:
Honest plain words best pierce the ear of grief.
~ *Love's Labor's Lost* (V.ii.753).

Show Me The Money

TIMEWORN:
Money talks.

REFRESHING:
They say, if money go before, all ways do lie open.
~ *The Merry Wives of Windsor* (II.ii.168-169).

When all of the trite thinkers of our time are insisting that "money talks," you are demonstrating your creative capacity to say exactly the same thing, but now with Shakespearean cachet.

OTHER COUPLETS – *It's All About The Benjamins*

COMMON:

Everyone's got a price.

TRANSFORMED:

Who so firm that cannot be seduced?

~ *Julius Caesar* (I.ii.312).

COMMON:

Now that he's rich, it's amazing how attractive he has become.

TRANSFORMED:

O, what a world of vile ill-favored faults
Looks handsome in three hundred pounds a year!

~ *The Merry Wives of Windsor* (III.iv.32-33).

[Note: Change "pounds" to "dollars" and make it six figures!]

CHAPTER 9.
Fifty Ways To Love Your Shakespeare

It's time to strut your stuff, as you explore a potpourri of life situations that lack only one thing to make them especially memorable: the perfect word or image. Now, thanks to your newfound Shakespearean virtuosity, you'll capture these moments with an amazing display of elegance and class. This is sure to drive all of your friends and loved ones crazy. It doesn't get any sweeter.

1. Playing The Wise Philosopher

BORE EVERYONE:
There's a time for everything.

OR BRING SOME REAL ZEST:
**How many things by season seasoned are
To their right praise and true perfection!**
~ *The Merchant of Venice* (V.i.107-108).

It was not without some trepidation that I used this quote on a card to a dear friend on the occasion of her 50th birthday. She must have appreciated it, however, because she did not season my soup with strychnine at her next dinner party. This may or may not be a source of comfort to purchasers of this book.

2. Mocking The Blowhard

HOW DRY:

I'm sick of hearing his/her voice.

HOW DROLL:

He gives the bastinado with his tongue;
Our ears are cudgelled.

~ *King John* (II.i.463-464).

To "give the bastinado" refers to beating someone with a stick. Of course, you can change "the bastinado" to something like "a thrashing" but it does lose something in the translation. Change it or not, the quote is an excellent insult for those annoying characters who dearly love to beat others about the ears with verbiage. Now you can do some cudgeling of your own with a fine Shakespearean flair.

3. Scorning The Bore

SELF-PITYING NONSENSE:

I'd rather shoot myself.

SELF-AFFIRMING CONFIDENCE:

I had rather live
With cheese and garlic in a windmill, far,
Than feed on cates and have him talk to me
In any summer house in Christendom.

~ *Henry IV, Part One* (III.i.159-162).

The notion of living on "cheese and garlic in a windmill" is too marvelous to pass up. Feeding on "cates," which means delicacies, and living in a summer house can readily be changed to fit a variety of circumstances, such as "than work one more day with those fools" or "than spend another five minutes with that idiot."

> [Note: Of course, change "Christendom" to the location of your choice, for example, Jersey Shore, Colorado or Vancouver.]

4. Insulting The Windbag

SHORT AND VULGAR:
What a blabbermouth.

LONG AND CLEVER:
[He] speaks an infinite deal of nothing, more than any man in all Venice. His reasons are as two grains of wheat hid in two bushels of chaff; you shall seek all day ere you find them, and when you have them, they are not worth the search.
~ *The Merchant of Venice* (I.i.114-118).

Changing Venice to the location of your choice, you will find these words a nicely framed insult directed at the Uncle and Aunt Gabbies of this world. This quote won't stop their chatter, of course; but their efforts to decipher its meaning will at least slow them down a bit.

5. Disdaining The Pampered

TROT OUT THE INSIPID:
Spoiled rotten.

OR SAGELY SUGGEST:
Dulled and cloyed with gracious favors.
~ *Henry V* (II.ii.9).

Their rich father indulges the twins next door to the point of absurdity. They have become the world-weariest teenagers you know and are thoroughly jaded by life's pleasures. Now you have the description, if helpless to effect the cure.

6. Listening Attentively

LAMELY MENTION:

I heard you loud and clear.

OR BOLDLY ANNOUNCE:

Your tale, sir, would cure deafness.

~ *The Tempest* (I.ii.106).

I happen to enjoy the friendship of a wonderful larger-than-life character who, with robust voice, loves to regale his friends with lively stories of past adventures. As he tells his tales, his "Are you listening?" (often accompanied by a very friendly but never-to-be-forgotten flying elbow to the ribs) is already the stuff of legend. Well, if you have the pleasure to know such a person, you may want to respond to his or her query with the very assuring "Your tale, dear friend, would cure deafness." Then again, you may not be paying much attention, in which case you will want to protect your flanks!

7. Giving Romance Its Due

SINK INTO BLANDNESS:

It's worth all the grief to be with her.

OR RISE TO THE OCCASION:

Come what sorrow can,
It cannot countervail the exchange of joy
That one short minute gives me in her sight.

~ *Romeo and Juliet* (II.vi.3-5).

158

Everyone seems to be against your new romance. And stage-whispered comments like "high maintenance," "too possessive," and the ever popular "what could they possibly have in common" are annoying evidence of where your friends stand on the subject. But you refuse to let all this negativity derail a wonderful relationship. When a friend marvels at your resolve in the face of such an onslaught of disapproval, you respond with an adjusted version of the above quote, to wit, "As the Bard says, all this criticism counts for nothing compared to 'the exchange of joy that one short minute gives me in her (or his) sight.'"

8. Resisting Temptation

JOIN THE HERD:
I don't give in to temptation.

OR STAY ABOVE THE CROWD:
'Tis one thing to be tempted...
Another thing to fall.
~ *Measure for Measure* (II.i.17-18).

You have just returned from your once-in-a-lifetime trip to the Riviera – on business, of course. Wide-eyed and envious, your friend queries, "All of those fabulous bodies, all of those temptations, how could you resist straying from the straight and narrow." "Don't be ridiculous," you respond with just the right touch of moral outrage. "I'm impervious to such enticements. Remember the words of the Bard, 'Tis one thing to be tempted, another thing to fall.'"

9. Sounding The Scoundrel Alarm

THEY'LL YAWN WHEN THEY HEAR:
Men are cads.

NOW YOU HAVE THEIR ATTENTION:
Sigh no more, ladies, sigh no more,
Men were deceivers ever,
One foot in sea, and one on shore,
To one thing constant never.
~ *Much Ado About Nothing* (II.iii.62-65).

and

We are arrant knaves, believe none of us.
Go thy ways to a nunnery.
~ *Hamlet* (III.i.128-129).

Some guys just don't know when they have a good thing. To make your point to your girlfriends you can launch into a vigorous "Sigh no more…" and be quite convincing. Or you can tune in to more simple advice to the lovelorn or the jilted: "Men are arrant knaves all: believe none of them. Let's get ourselves to Bloomingdales!"

10. Inviting Intimacy

NO ONE'S LISTENING:
For your ears only.

NOW THEY'RE EAGER:
For I would commune with you of such things
That want no ear but yours.
~ *Measure for Measure* (IV.iii.104-105).

You've been away from home at a conference all week, talking business with a group of distinctly tiresome characters. What a great time to send an e-mail to your honey with the above quote. You may want to add: "These boors are boring me to tears. I can't wait to get home and get down to more important business – spending time with my sweetie."

11. Embracing Ecstasy

PEDESTRIAN:
You're head over heels in love.

REMARKABLE:
You are already Love's firm votary.
~ *The Two Gentlemen of Verona* (III.ii.58).

Your chums cannot help but notice: no more booze parties, no more all night poker sessions, and no more flatulence contests. Something is drastically wrong and they demand to know what. Your retort is concise: "The answer is simple. I've fallen madly in love. In fact, I am already 'love's firm votary'." Do not be offended, however, if those who know you best do not immediately cancel your reservations to the annual Suds Ahoy beer bash. This maturation thing can be a slow process.

12. Denouncing A Cad

COMMON WARNING:
Beware of the smooth talker.

ELEGANT ADMONITION:
These fellows of infinite tongue, that can rhyme themselves into ladies' favors, they do always reason themselves out again.
~ *Henry V* (V.ii.155-158).

That menace from apartment 3B has been trying to move in on your girlfriend with a veritable arsenal of clever sayings and poetic come-ons. He thinks he is so suave; but you see right through him, of course. Despite your best efforts at sabotage, however, he may be starting to make some headway. Something has to be done quickly, and you know exactly what it is. On a beautiful card, you pen this sage, if self-serving, Shakespearean advice, "These slicksters of infinite tongue, that can rhyme themselves into a lady's favor, they do always reason themselves out again." You then add, "I, on the other hand, am here for the long haul and need only the original smoothie, William Shakespeare, to make my point."

13. Walking On Air

STAY EARTH-BOUND:

When you are in love you're on cloud nine.

OR REALLY FIND YOUR WINGS:

A lover may bestride the gossamers
That idles in the wanton summer air,
And yet not fall.

~ *Romeo and Juliet* (II.vi.18-20).

You've had a wonderful time once again with your lover and it's time for some formal acknowledgement. With the Bard's help and perhaps the appropriate floral arrangement, you've got the perfect touch. The card presents the entire Shakespearean quote; and then you add this helpful translation: "Now I know what it means to be walking on air."

14. Making Up Passionately

NO OOMPH:
Making up sure is great.

PERFECT:
O my soul's joy!
If after every tempest come such calms,
May the winds blow till they have wakened death!
~ *Othello* (II.i.184-186).

It sure was a doozy of an argument! But when the storm clouds had passed, it was quite the sweet make-up session that followed. Later you send an e-mail: "We certainly know how to argue, but we're even better at making up. As Shakespeare said, 'If after every tempest comes such calms, may the winds blow till they have wakened death!' Why don't you come by at seven so we can 'argue' some more."

15. Hiding The Truth

CREATE TEDIUM WITH:
She never said how much she loved him.

OR SHOW SOME STYLE:
She never told her love,
But let concealment like a worm in the bud,
Feed on her damask cheek.
~ *Twelfth Night* (II.iv.110-112).

Your friend has been in love with a really sweet guy for a number of years now; but, given the poor fellow's cluelessness, she continues to play her hand far too coyly. You can't stand it anymore and decide to do what everyone agrees you do best: Butt in. So, armed with the master's incomparable imagery, you proceed to make your point, taking care to change "damask" (which, in this context, is the color pink) to something like "lovely," since most people don't have the foggiest idea what damask means.

16. Engaging The Romantic Battle

TIRESOMELY PROCLAIM:

All's fair in love and war.

OR WISELY ANNOUNCE:

**Friendship is constant in all other things
Save in the office and affairs of love.**

~ *Much Ado About Nothing* (II.i.175-176).

There is nothing like some spirited competition between friends for the same object of affection. Yes, it's true: You just met the perfect man or woman of your dreams, and the only cloud in this silver lining is the fact that one of your friends has designs on the same heartthrob. Don't back down from the duel of love. Instead throw down the gauntlet with Shakespearean class. Send an e-mail featuring the above quote, to which you add, "Let the battle commence."

17. Dispensing Praise

SPARE US THE STERILE:
I'll never be able to repay you.

AND MAKE GRATITUDE SUBLIME:

Would thou hadst less deserved,
That the proportion both of thanks and payment
Might have been mine!
Only I have left to say,
More is thy due than more than all can pay.

~ *Macbeth* (I.iv.18-21).

One of my all-time favorite quotes. I've personally used it on several occasions: once, many years ago, for a luncheon toast for a truly superb co-worker who was moving to another job; and, more recently, at an anniversary for ten-year veterans at my workplace. The whole quote is great and surprisingly easy to remember; but, if you prefer brevity, use only the last two lines and you will still have a marvelous toast.

18. Delivering A Classy Send-Off

SO HACKNEYED:
The cruise is quite pleasant.

SO INVENTIVE:
The wind sits in the shoulder of your sail.

~ *Hamlet* (I.iii.56).

It used to be that the task of toasting a couple at their wedding before they set out on their honeymoon cruise would have filled you with dread. And, admit it, the sad fact is that the ever tedious "bon voyage" might well have punctuated your thoroughly forgettable remarks. But that was yesterday and today is Shakespeare. So now you give the newlyweds a memorable send-off with "May the wind sit in the shoulder of your sail." Conventional bore or clever toastmaster – the choice is yours.

19. Decrying Indifference

REJECT THE FAMILIAR:
He's never felt the pain we feel.

EMBRACE THE EXTRAORDINARY:
He jests at scars that never felt a wound.
~ *Romeo and Juliet* (II.ii.1).

Sadly, there will always be people in this world whose sole response to a painful event in someone else's life will be the ever popular "It couldn't be that bad." Now, when you hear these obnoxious words, you will have the perfect Shakespearean retort.

20. Reaffirming Your Affection

CRUDELY STATE:
We sure were hot that night.

OR POETICALLY INSIST:
Eternity was in our lips and eyes,
Bliss in our brows' bent; none our parts so poor
But was a race of heaven.
~ *Antony and Cleopatra* (I.iii.35-37).

It's time to rekindle the passion. What better way to kick things off than to send a bouquet of flowers or a special gift to your lover's office or home with the above marvelous sentiment. Since the quote, although terrific, can benefit from some adjustment to suit the modern taste, feel free to employ the following rendition: "Remember how we were when we first met. Eternity was in our lips and eyes, bliss in our kisses, and no caress so poor but was a gift from heaven. Let's spice things up a bit with a wonderful weekend in the Bahamas."

21. Challenging A Foe

CRASSLY YELL:

Turn around, you coward.

OR STOUTLY DEMAND:

Turn, hell-hound, turn!

~ *Macbeth* (V.viii.3).

"Obviously he is a stranger to these parts," you say to your friend, as a young upstart presumes to question your well-known mastery of verbal fisticuffs. The insolent whelp then compounds the insult by leaving the scene of battle with an arrogant saunter. "Turn, hell-hound, turn," you say, as you prepare to teach the presumptuous puppy what clever argumentation is all about. The very idea!

22. Arriving At Wisdom

OLD AS IN MUSTY:

To get wise as one gets grey with age.

OLD AS IN RIPENED TO PERFECTION:

To achieve
The silver livery of advised age.

~ *Henry VI, Part Two* (V.ii.46-47).

It's the retirement party for good old Bill, with his perfectly preserved grey head of hair; and everyone is going to give him thoroughly respectable and totally forgettable gifts to commemorate it. Not you. You buy a beautiful silver scarf, place it in a distinctive box, and include a card with the following words, "Now that you have achieved the 'silver livery of advised age,' it seems appropriate to give you something to symbolize your elevated state." It's true that Bill may not have a clue as to what "silver livery" means (a reference to the white hair of persons of a certain age), but he'll know a classy gift when he sees one.

23. Gushing With Enthusiasm

A GOOEY EMBARRASSMENT:
Wow is this great!

A BUOYANT SURPRISE:

O, rejoice
Beyond a common joy, and set it down
With gold on lasting pillars.
~ *The Tempest* (V.i.206-208).

There are times when you're in the mood for some shameless, unrestrained enthusiasm. When you are so inclined, let everybody else hold forth with their lackluster renditions of "golly gee," "wow" and "isn't this great." You know how to gush with panache.

24. Celebrating Courage

TRUE BUT TAME:

One gutsy lady.

TRUE AND CAPTIVATING:

O tiger's heart wrapp'd in a woman's hide!
~ *Henry VI, Part Three* (I.iv.137).

You have just witnessed your friend do battle against the powers that be because she would not compromise her principles. You can't resist leaving a little note where you know she will see it, changing "hide" to "skin." With the above quote prominently featured, you extol her courage and express your admiration. Emulating her bold behavior is optional.

25. Meeting Calamity Head-On

NO SPICE:

What's cookin'.

JUST THE RIGHT SEASONING:

Double, double, toil and trouble;
Fire burn, and cauldron bubble.
~ *Macbeth* (IV.i.10-11).

Your husband or boyfriend is determined to make dinner for you on Valentine's Day. You come into the kitchen to observe how things are going and see catastrophe staring you in the face. Performing lead roles in this culinary disaster, the pasta is boiling over and the garlic bread is on its way to a fine blackened crisp. It's time for you to gently put your hand on his shoulder, utter the immortal words of the witches in Macbeth, and provide some much-needed assistance. Then again you may want to pretend you've seen nothing at all, return to the comfort of the den, and take a long, lingering sip of a delicious chardonnay. Decisions, decisions.

26. Promoting Leisure

YOU'LL PUT THEM TO SLEEP WITH:

Go and take it easy.

OR PUT A BOUNCE IN THEIR STEP:

Time be thine,
And thy best graces spend it at thy will!
~ *Hamlet* (I.ii.62-63).

On so many levels your mate has been a terrific support all week. So, by way of saying thanks, you place the above quote on a special card with the promise that you'll take over his or her portion of household chores for an entire week... But wait a minute. Perhaps one shouldn't be too hasty. How about using the same quote but giving a gift certificate to Starbucks instead? Now that's a promise that would be considerably less trying on your best graces!

27. Criticizing A Nasty Tongue

RUN FOR COVER:

She's got quite the mouth.

BUT NOT BEFORE YOU SAY THIS:

She speaks poniards, and every word stabs.
If her breath were as terrible as her terminations,
there were no living near her,
she would infect to the north star.
~ *Much Ado About Nothing* (II.i.247-250).

It grieves you to say it, but your friend's girlfriend has quite a barbed tongue. When another friend asks your opinion of the prickly lady, you can't resist employing the Bard with some modern adjustment: "She speaks daggers and every word stabs. If her breath were as terrible as her tongue lashings, there would be no living near her, she would infect to the North Star." Need we say that this quote can easily be gender adjusted? Yes, we need.

28. Chiding Inconsiderate Offspring

TRUTH IS ON YOUR SIDE:
What an ungrateful brat!

SO CHIDE IN STYLE:
**How sharper than a serpent's tooth it is
To have a thankless child!**
~ *King Lear* (I.iv.288-289).

Let's construct a scenario so far fetched that no parent of a teenage son or daughter will have the slightest idea what I'm talking about. Now let's see. Formerly a source of delight, the teenager in question now seems to be settling into the role of thoughtless, ungrateful, lazy brat. He or she won't do a thing around the house but make a total mess of his or her room and be on the computer or smartphone every waking moment. Finally, you've had enough, and after some outrageous act of thoughtlessness, you utter the above quote, punctuating your remarks with a shake of the finger that would split a tree stump. How's that for sheer fantasy?

29. Faking Contentment

BLANDLY ADMIT YOUR DISGUISE:

I'm hiding behind a smile.

OR CLEVERLY REVEAL IT:

I show more mirth than I am mistress of.

~ *As You Like It* (I.ii.3-4).

Your husband's Uncle Fred has just invited himself for a two-week visit, the same Uncle Fred who loves to make snide references to what he views as your cooking and housekeeping deficiencies. Oh, yes, and did I mention that he's bringing his complete set of Three Stooges movies for your nightly viewing pleasure? The apparently happy front you try to put on at dinner, after hearing the news, has not gone unnoticed by your teenage children. They inquire as to why you seem so cheerful, given Uncle Fred's imminent arrival. Thanks to the Bard, your answer is short and concise. Your plans for the slow, agonizing demise of the dear fellow would take longer to discuss, were you inclined to share them.

30. Staying Above It All

CREATE APATHY:

He's very self-disciplined.

OR SPUR REFLECTION:

One who never feels
The wanton stings and motions of the sense;
But doth rebate and blunt his natural edge
With profits of the mind: study and fast.

~ *Measure for Measure* (I.iv.58-61).

The suggestion has been made (by those who have yet to grasp his inner essence) that your friend is little more than a walking lust machine. This slander cannot go unchallenged. Your response, a model of righteous indignation, goes something like this: "Yes, as all mortals, he is not immune to the 'wanton stings and motions' of his senses; but he continually strives to oppose this inclination with 'profits of the mind, study and fast.'" What a marvelous, Shakespeare-to-the-rescue friend – deluded, but marvelous!

31. Being True To Yourself

GOOD ADVICE:
Always be honest with yourself.

NOW ADD SOME FLAIR:
To thine own self be true,
And it must follow, as the night the day,
Thou canst not then be false to any man.
~ *Hamlet* (I.iii.78-80).

Always be true to yourself is great advice to live by, and now the Bard enables you to make the point with true panache. It's true that the speaker of these words, Polonius, was a bit of a windbag; but this slice of wisdom, so perceptive and pithy, only goes to prove that we can all rise above our natures from time to time. For some reason this quote has always been a source of comfort to me.

32. Going With Your Gut

IF YOU CAN'T FIND ANY LOGIC:
It makes no sense to do it.

AT LEAST FIND A GOOD METAPHOR:
My reason
Sits in the wind against me.
~ *Antony and Cleopatra* (III.x.35-36).

These words were spoken by the soldier Enobarbus when contemplating whether or not he should leave the service of his friend Mark Antony. Perhaps you will be in a similar situation, like trying to decide whether or not to go bungee jumping when everyone and your own good sense tell you that you're insane. So when the time comes, just say, "I'm going to do it, though my reason sits in the wind against me." It's true that things didn't work out very well for Enobarbus (he dies, it would seem, of a broken heart!), but is there any doubt that your skill and courage will bring you through unscathed?

33. Challenging Narrow Thinking

TOO CONSTRICTED:
You're too limited in your perceptions.

BREADTH TO SPARE:
There are more things in heaven and earth, Horatio,
Than are dreamt of in your philosophy.
~ *Hamlet* (I.v.166-167).

This is one of the more famous two-liners in Shakespeare. It's great for that moment when someone obnoxiously insists that he or she knows what ultimate truth is. A good friend of mine assures me, however, that a famous philosopher once was confronted with this very quote from the Bard and had a clever rejoinder, "I just want to make sure that there is not more in my philosophy than there is in heaven and on earth."

34. Bursting An Overconfident Bubble

YOU NEED BETTER PACKAGING:
Don't overestimate what you have to offer.

HERE'S THE RIGHT WRAPPING:
Sell when you can, you are not for all markets.
~ *As You Like It* (III.v.60).

You really love your friend Sam, and he is indeed a great guy. But, truth be told, his girlfriends have been few and far between. But now he has met a terrific person who seems to truly appreciate him for who he is, warts and all. Marriage seemed imminent; but now, sadly, he has started to have second thoughts. He's hinting about her not being "perfect enough." You try to hold your tongue but, of course, fail miserably to do so. After employing the above words from Shakespeare to get his attention, here is how you conclude: "Don't blow this opportunity for happiness because of some impossible standards for a mate. She's a great person and, let's face it, you are not exactly a love magnet." Gad you're good – quite the buttinsky – but good.

35. Rationalizing Bad Behavior

YOU'VE HEARD THIS BEFORE:

I'm only doing my job.

BUT NOT THIS:

Why, ... 'tis my vocation, ... 'tis no sin
for a man to labor in his vocation.

~ *Henry IV, Part One* (I.ii.104-105).

Falstaff used these words in reference to his own purse-taking proclivities. Fortunately your behavior is not of a criminal nature. Still an increasing number of people are finding your total preoccupation with golf quite annoying. "But I am retired now," you insist, "and golf is my new career." So, when these busybodies complain about your constant visits to the links, you smugly nip their moral scolding in the bud with this clever Shakespearean rationale for your new "vocation." And all is peachy keen in your comfy little world until your reverie is interrupted by the dulcet tones of your beloved wife reminding you of today's "honey-do" list. Apparently your new vocation comes with a new supervisor, and she has her own ideas as to what is a sin and what is not.

36. Finishing What You've Started

POORLY DONE INDEED:

We're not done with our work.

SO MUCH BETTER:

We have scorched the snake, not killed it;
She'll close and be herself, whilst our poor malice
Remains in danger of her former tooth.

~ *Macbeth* (III.ii.13-15).

Don't confuse weakening the opposition with actually destroying it. Or so goes the sentiment of this quote, which is ideal for the times when your sporting efforts have only succeeded in stunning rather than thoroughly trouncing your foe. Utilizing the quote does require a little work, however, because "scorched" should be changed to something like "wounded"; and "close" should be changed to "heal." With these minor changes, however, you really do have an effective quotation, and you must admit that the last phrase "whilst our poor malice remains in danger of her former tooth" is a real gem. At the very least you're sure to get a few quick points while the bewildered and eavesdropping opposition tries to figure out what on earth you are talking about.

37. Showing Good Judgment

JOIN THE CLICHÉ CLUB WITH:
Fools rush in where angels fear to tread.

OR RIP UP YOUR MEMBERSHIP CARD:
**But modest doubt is called
The beacon of the wise.**

~ *Troilus and Cressida* (II.ii.15-16).

Everyone's stampeding to judgment regarding the alleged indiscretion of your co-worker; but you calmly suggest that a healthy skepticism be maintained: "Since 'modest doubt is called the beacon of the wise,' I'll wait for further information before drawing any final conclusion." Guess who is proven to be the wise one when all the facts are in?

38. Putting Yourself In God's Hands

GOD SHIELDING:
I'm under the Almighty's protection.

GOD CHERISHING:
In the great hand of God I stand.
~ *Macbeth* (II.iii.130).

Changing "I" to "we," you have a very appropriate quote for a sympathy card to a friend who has just suffered a terrible loss. The entire card may read something like this: "There are no adequate words of comfort at such a time. In the great hand of God we stand."

39. Loving In A Balanced Way

CHOOSE PSYCHOLOGICAL PABLUM:
You've got to love yourself first.

OR GRADUATE TO REAL FOOD:
Self-love ... is not so vile a sin
As self-neglecting.
~ *Henry V* (II.iv.74).

One of the tenets of modern psychology is that we are not sufficiently attentive to our own needs. The truth is often a bit more complicated than that, and this quote captures the nuance quite nicely.

40. Confronting Terror

NOTHING INTERESTING HERE:
What a bunch of weirdos!

I TAKE IT BACK:
Hell is empty,
And all the devils are here.
~ *The Tempest* (I.ii.214-215).

You are about to enter the room where twelve seven-year olds are preparing to celebrate a birthday party. Your compatriot in this act of insanity can't help but notice your trepidation. She insists that they are little angels once you get to know them. "I am sure they are," you warily respond, as you open the door to the blood-curdling sound of the little monsters yelling and screaming to their hearts content. As sheer terror envelopes your usually quite amiable countenance, you cannot help but exclaim, "Hell is empty and all the little devils are here."

41. Discovering Your Own Pain

DO MORE THAN THINK:
You've got me reflecting on my own pain.

FIND THE RIGHT WORDS:
Searching of thy wound,
I have by hard adventure found mine own.
~ *As You Like It* (II.iv.44-45).

Trying to be the helpful counselor does have its drawbacks. You may experience, for example, the discomfort of becoming reacquainted with your own pain while exploring the heartache of someone else. Of course, this may well result in your attaining greater wisdom and compassion. Then again, it may just bum you out and make you grumpy, in which case being able to quote the Bard to the admiration of all may prove to be the perfect medicine.

42. Skewering Expertise

UNINSPIRED:
You're supposed to be the experts, not them.
PERCEPTIVE:
What your wisdoms could not discover,
these shallow fools have brought to light.
~ *Much Ado About Nothing* (V.i.232-234).

Few pleasures can equal the sheer joy of watching pompous, so-called experts make fools of themselves. When this happens, "shallow fools" can be changed to "little children," "simple folks," "ordinary citizens" or whatever fits the circumstances. Try not to look too smug when you say it.

43. Grumbling About Your Job

ABANDON THIS LABORED PHRASE:
This job is the pits.
AND CHOOSE A DELIGHTFUL ALTERNATIVE:
O how full of briers is this working-day world!
~ *As You Like It* (I.iii.11-12).

As you drag your sad behind to work on Monday morning, you find yourself muttering the above quote to your equally cranky co-workers. Or, much worse, while seated on your accustomed Friday night perch at the local bistro, you find yourself uttering these words of lament after receiving the bad news that someone else got the promotion.

44. Seeking Liquid Solace

STALE BEER:
I need a drink.

RARE BREW:
I will see what physic the tavern affords.
~ *Henry VI, Part One* (III.i.146).

It's been a bad day on the links and you need some balm to salve your dejected spirit. Turning to your chums you recall Shakespeare's immortal words, "Let's repair to Charlie's Saloon and 'see what physic the tavern affords.'"

45. Grieving A Loss

SOOTHING, AS IN SEDATING:
She looks so peaceful.

PIERCING TO THE HEART:
Death lies on her like an untimely frost
Upon the sweetest flower in all the field.
~ *Romeo and Juliet* (IV.v.28-29).

On the occasion of an untimely death, particularly of one who is young, this quote on a card with accompanying personal words of condolence is quite moving. Whether it is to mourn the death of a child or to comment on the death of a young person full of promise, the world offers far too many opportunities to use these poignant words.

46. Focusing On What You Love

SAY WHAT THEY ALL SAY:

Study what gives you pleasure.

OR MAKE IT MEMORABLE:

No profit grows where is no pleasure taken.
In brief, sir, study what you most affect.

~ *The Taming of the Shrew* (I.i.39-40).

Away with this "no pain, no gain" routine. To paraphrase George Bernard Shaw, as he responded to an inquiry regarding the secret of his long life, "Find out what you really love to do and then dive in." The advice served him well; but then again, as a tireless writer, who was also a tea-totaling vegetarian, he was one fellow who really needed to enjoy his work.

47. Taking The Mature Approach

BE EVER SO OBVIOUS:

I know what's best because I'm older and wiser.

OR EVER SO CRAFTY:

[I have] a purpose
More grave and wrinkled than the aims and ends
Of burning youth.

~ *Measure for Measure* (I.iii.4-6).

For reasons of generosity and kindness you want to be chosen over another volunteer as organizer of this year's annual charity dinner. "Her goals for the event betray her inexperience and immaturity," you insist, as you comment on the candidacy of Marie, your young and quite attractive competitor. Changing "wrinkled" (good heavens!) to something far more suitable, you continue your analysis: "I on the other hand have a purpose more grave and seasoned than the aims and ends of burning youth." After your brilliant turn of a Shakespearean phrase has secured your election, you will proceed to the arrangements. Be sure to seat yourself next to the guest speaker. For all of his wealth and rugged good looks, he is an unattached and reportedly lonely fellow who will need a woman of your maturity and judgment to see him through the festivities and any subsequent activities. Such a complex and sophisticated agenda is something that the "less grave" Marie would surely not have been able to handle.

48. Letting Others Shine

SOUND LIKE A LOSER:
You'll look great in comparison to me.

OR WIN BEFORE YOU START:

I'll be your foil ... in mine ignorance
Your skill shall like a star in the darkest night
Stick fiery off indeed.
~ *Hamlet* (V.ii.255-257).

Like Hamlet, you are about to enter into a competition where you are a decided underdog. Rather than puff yourself up and start talking trash, you employ the above quote instead. Not only will you appear to be the classier competitor; but also, in case you are thoroughly trounced, you will gain a reputation for graciousness. Of course, this is not nearly as good as winning, but it beats being perceived as a whiny loser.

49. Making Blissful Love Again

THE MOMENT'S TOO GOOD FOR:
I want to spend one more night with him or her.

SO CHOOSE THE REFINED:

Hold off the earth awhile,
Till I have caught her once more in mine arms.
~ *Hamlet* (V.i.249-250).

You are scheduled to return to work on Monday from a great romantic weekend. But you have just come up with a much better idea. Your e-mail, gender adjusted to taste, beautifully informs your co-workers of a change of plans: "Will arrive one day later. Have decided, as Shakespeare said, to 'hold off the earth awhile, 'till I have caught her/him once more in my arms.'"

AND FINALLY:

50. Finding The Sweetness

YOU COULD INSIST ON THE BROMIDIC:
Hard experience is the best teacher.

OR CHOOSE A TRUE ORIGINAL INSTEAD:
Sweet are the uses of adversity.
~ *As You Like It* (II.i.12).

It is a Shakespearean sweetness of remarkable versatility, and it doesn't need to be attached to hardship at all. Quite the contrary. For example, you could say, "Sweet are the uses of a summer holiday," "Sweet are the uses of a water bed," or "Sweet are the uses of hot fudge." You might even say, "Sweet are the uses of this book" – and that would be sweet indeed.

Index To Key Words And Phrases

abusing of God's patience
~ *The Merry Wives of Windsor*
(I.iv.4-6), 48

accidental evils
~ *Julius Caesar* (IV.iii.146), 144

adders fanged
~ *Hamlet* (III.iv.203), 52

adversity's sweet milk
~ *Romeo and Juliet* (III.iii.55), 148

age cannot wither her
~ *Antony and Cleopatra*
(II.ii.234-237), 9

air hath starved the roses
~ *The Two Gentlemen of Verona*
(IV.iv.154-155), 40

alacrity in sinking
~ *The Merry Wives of Windsor*
(III.v.12-13), 102

all the world's a stage
~ *As You Like It* (II.vii.139-140), 117

angels and ministers of grace
~ *Hamlet* (I.iv.39), 139

arrant knaves
~ *Hamlet* (III.i.128-129), 160

assurance of a man
~ *Hamlet* (III.iv.60-62), 92

bastinado with his tongue
~ *King John* (II.i.463-464), 156

bawdy planet
~ *The Winter's Tale* (I.ii.201), 14

beauty did astonish
~ *All's Well That Ends Well*
(V.iii.15-19), 58

beauty truly blent
~ *Twelfth Night* (I.v.239-240), 33

beauty's ensign
~ *Romeo and Juliet* (V.iii.94-95), 32

beg often our own harms
~ *Antony and Cleopatra* (II.i.5-8), 139

beggared all description
~ *Antony and Cleopatra* (II.ii.197-198), 27

beguile the lazy time
~ *A Midsummer Night's Dream*
(V.i.40-41), 94

beguile the thing I am
~ *Othello* (II.i.122-123), 81

begun to plant thee
~ *Macbeth* (I.iv.28-29), 84

best graces spend
~ *Hamlet* (I.ii.62-63), 170

best men are moulded
~ *Measure for Measure* (V.i.439-441), 145

best safety
~ *Hamlet* (I.iii.43), 80

better a little chiding
~ *The Merry Wives of Windsor*
(V.iii.9-10), 66

beware ... of jealousy
~ *Othello* (III.iii.165-167), 15

blackest sins put on
~ *Othello* (II.iii.351-352), 80

blessed ministers above
~ *Measure for Measure* (V.i.115-116), 151

blessed spirit doth speak
~ *All's Well That Ends Well* (II.i.175), 139

blest are those whose blood and judgment
~ Hamlet (III.ii.68-71), 39

blood burns, how prodigal
~ Hamlet (I.iii.116-117), 22

blood in his belly that will sup a flea
~ Love's Labor's Lost (V.ii.691-692), 50

blow, blow, thou winter wind
~ As You Like it (II.vii.174-176), 113

blurs the grace and blush of modesty
~ Hamlet (III.iv.40-41), 113

bold and saucy wrongs
~ Othello (I.i.128), 65

boldness of my cunning
~ Measure for Measure (IV.ii.155-156), 104

book, wherein my soul recorded
~ Richard III (III.v.27-28), 70

bosom shall partake
~ Julius Caesar (II.i.305-306), 70

bosom up my counsel
~ Henry VIII (I.i.112-113), 85

boy eternal
~ The Winter's Tale (I.ii.63-64), 68

braggart shall be found an ass
~ All's Well That Ends Well (IV.iii.335-336), 46

brave new world
~ The Tempest (V.i.182-184), 98

breach in his abused nature
~ King Lear (IV.vii.14-15), 64

brightness of her cheek
~ Romeo and Juliet (II.ii.19-20), 33

brimstone in your liver
~ Twelfth Night (III.ii.20-21), 93

brooch indeed and gem
~ Hamlet (IV.vii.94), 36

candle singed the moth
~ The Merchant of Venice (II.ix.79), 151

candy deal of courtesy
~ Henry IV, Part One (I.iii.251-252), 75

canker that eats up
~ Venus and Adonis (656), 16

cheese and garlic in a windmill
~ Henry IV, Part One (III.i.159-162), 156

choice and master spirits
~ Julius Caesar (III.i.163), 37

come what sorrow can
~ Romeo and Juliet (II.vi.3-5), 158

comfort like to this
~ Othello (II.i.189-193), 57

comfort's in heaven
~ Richard II (II.ii.78-79), 103

commune with you
~ Measure for Measure (IV.iii.104-105), 160

compare thee to a summer's day
~ Sonnet 18 (1-2), 17

constant in spirit
~ Henry V (II.ii.133), 38

contended especially to know himself
~ Measure for Measure (III.ii.232-233), 141

cool and temperate wind of grace
~ Henry V (III.iii.30), 35

cool our raging motions
~ Othello (I.iii.335), 14

course of true love
~ *A Midsummer Night's Dream*
(I.i.134), 23

cowards die many times
~ *Julius Caesar* (II.ii.32-33), 108

cozening hope
~ *Richard II* (II.ii.68-69), 101

crack of doom
~ *Macbeth* (IV.i.117), 42

crown and comfort of my life
~ *The Winter's Tale* (III.ii.94), 19

cunning past man's thought
~ *Antony and Cleopatra* (I.ii.145), 74

**curb her mad and
headstrong humor**
~ *The Taming of the Shrew* (IV.i.209), 66

cure deafness
~ *The Tempest* (I.ii.106), 158

curse of marriage
~ *Othello* (III.iii.268-270), 60

daily beauty in his life
~ *Othello* (V.i.19-20), 31

danger knows full well
~ *Julius Caesar* (II.ii.44-45), 109

**dare do all that may become
a man**
~ *Macbeth* (I.vii.46-47), 107

dare not call them fools
~ *Love's Labor's Lost* (V.ii.371-372), 45

dauntless temper of his mind
~ *Macbeth* (III.i.49-53), 38

death lies on her
~ *Romeo and Juliet* (IV.v.28-29), 181

deceit should dwell
~ *Romeo and Juliet* (III.ii.83-84), 41

deceit should steal
~ *Richard III* (II.ii.27-28), 42

depth of this knavery
~ *The Taming of the Shrew* (V.i.137), 68

desert speaks loud
~ *Measure for Measure* (V.i.9-13), 82

desolate shade
~ *Macbeth* (IV.iii.1-2), 20

detraction at your heels
~ *Twelfth Night* (II.v.136-138), 80

devil can cite Scripture
~ *The Merchant of Venice* (I.iii.98), 81

devoted and given up himself
~ *Othello* (II.iii.316-318), 18

died in virtue's cause
~ *Titus Andronicus* (I.i.390), 124

discretion be your tutor
~ *Hamlet* (III.ii.16-17), 142

divinity that shapes our ends
~ *Hamlet* (V.ii.10-11), 139

dolor of the heart
~ *Richard II* (I.iii.255-257), 128

done, when 'tis done
~ *Macbeth* (I.vii.1-2), 112

doomsday is near
~ *Henry IV, Part One* (IV.i.134), 129

doubt thou the stars are fire
~ *Hamlet* (II.ii.116-119), 11

down, down I come
~ *Richard II* (III.iii.178-183), 114

drink deep
~ *Hamlet* (I.ii.175), 140

drowsy syrups of the world
~ *Othello* (III.iii.330-333), 8

dulled and cloyed
~ *Henry V* (II.ii.9), 157

dust which the rude wind
~ *King Lear* (IV.ii.30-31), 52

duty past thy might
~ *Julius Caesar* (IV.iii.261), 85

eating canker dwells
~ *The Two Gentlemen of Verona* (I.i.42-43), 146

enchanting presence and discourse
~ *The Comedy of Errors* (III.ii.160-161), 34

encounter darkness as a bride
~ *Measure for Measure* (III.i.82-84), 129

end is purposed by the mighty gods
~ *Julius Caesar* (II.ii.26-27), 140

engluts and swallows other sorrows
~ *Othello* (I.iii.55-58), 125

engross his idle body
~ *Richard III* (III.vii.76-77), 120

eternity was in our lips and eyes
~ *Antony and Cleopatra* (I.iii.35-37), 166

every thing that grows holds in perfection
~ *Sonnet 15* (1-2), 137

excellent dissembling
~ *Antony and Cleopatra* (I.iii.78-80), 66

expectation and rose
~ *Hamlet* (III.i.152), 37

extremity for love
~ *Hamlet* (II.ii.189-190), 7

eye discourses
~ *Romeo and Juliet* (II.ii.13), 12

eyes in heaven
~ *Romeo and Juliet* (II.ii.20-22), 30

fading moment's mirth
~ *The Two Gentlemen of Verona* (I. i.29-31), 7

fair an outward and such stuff within
~ *Cymbeline* (I.i.22-23), 31

fair goddess Fortune
~ *Coriolanus* (I.v.20-21), 88

fair rose wither
~ *Richard II* (V.i.7-8), 40

fair virtue's gloss
~ *Love's Labor's Lost* (II.i.47), 146

fairer than my love
~ *Romeo and Juliet* (I.ii.92-93), 29

false sweet bait
~ *Much Ado About Nothing* (III.i.32-33), 121

falser than vows
~ *As You Like It* (III.v.73), 44

fare thee well, great heart
~ *Henry IV, Part One* (V.iv.87-93), 124

farewell the tranquil mind
~ *Othello* (III.iii.347-348), 6

fashion's own knight
~ *Love's Labor's Lost* (I.i.178), 36

father of some stratagem
~ *Henry IV, Part Two* (I.i.7-8), 67

fear no more the heat o' th' sun
~ *Cymbeline* (IV.ii.258-263), 133

feather for each wind that blows
~ *The Winter's Tale* (II.iii.154), 102

fellows of infinite tongue
~ *Henry V* (V.ii.155-158), 161

fine foot, straight leg, and quivering thigh
~ *Romeo and Juliet* (II.i.19-20), 27

firm that cannot be seduced
~ *Julius Caesar* (I.ii.312), 153

flame of love
~ *Hamlet* (IV.vii.114-115), 20

flash and outbreak of a fiery mind
~ *Hamlet* (II.i.33), 83

flies to wanton boys
~ *King Lear* (IV.i.36-37), 103

foil, be your
~ *Hamlet* (V.ii.255-257), 184

fool may you find... even to the world's pleasure
~ *All's Well That Ends Well* (II.iv.35-37), 51

foolish in our stands
~ *Coriolanus* (I.vi.2), 89

forbear to judge
~ *Henry VI, Part Two* (III.iii.31), 146

fortune and victory sit
~ *Richard III* (V.iii.79), 88

fortune brings in some boats
~ *Cymbeline* (IV.iii.46), 83

fortune means to men most good
~ *King John* (III.iv.120), 149

fortune shall cull forth
~ *King John* (II.i.391-392), 89

fortune's minion and her pride
~ *Henry IV, Part One* (I.i.83), 116

fortune's yoke
~ *Henry VI, Part Three* (III.iii.16-18), 131

foul and fair a day
~ *Macbeth* (I.iii.38), 83

framed as fruitful
~ *Othello* (II.iii.341-342), 26

framed in the prodigality
~ *Richard III* (I.ii.243), 26

free and open nature
~ *Othello* (I.iii.399-402), 46

friendship is constant
~ *Much Ado About Nothing* (II.i.175-176), 164

fruit of rashness
~ *Richard III* (II.i.135), 78

full of grief as age
~ *King Lear* (II.iv.272-273), 101

full of sorrows as the sea of sands
~ *The Two Gentlemen of Verona* (IV.iii.32-33), 125

full prospect of my hopes
~ *Twelfth Night* (III.iv.81-82), 93

function is smothered in surmise
~ *Macbeth* (I.iii.140), 75

gall and pinch
~ *Henry IV, Part One* (I.iii.228-229), 92

garland of the war
~ *Antony and Cleopatra* (IV.xv.64), 91

gentleness shall force
~ *As You Like It* (II.vii.102-103), 142

glass wherein the noble youth
~ *Henry IV,Part Two* (II.iii.21-22), 35

glisters through my rust
~ *The Winter's Tale* (III.ii.170-171), 82

glories and my state depose
~ *Richard II* (IV.i.192-193), 100

gods themselves throw incense
~ *King Lear* (V.iii.20-21), 131

good hanging prevents
~ *Twelfth Night* (I.v.19), 62

good leg will fall
~ *Henry V* (V.ii.159-163), 32

good night, sweet prince
~ *Hamlet* (V.ii.359-360), 132

grace was seated on this brow
~ *Hamlet* (III.iv.55), 34

great hand of God I stand
~ *Macbeth* (II.iii.130), 178

greyhounds in the slips
~ *Henry V* (III.i.31-32), 89

grief hath kept a tedious fast
~ *Richard II* (II.i.75), 100

grim necessity
~ *Richard II* (V.i.20-22), 100

grown in grace
~ *The Winter's Tale* (IV.i.24-25), 35

gypsy's lust
~ *Antony and Cleopatra* (I.i.9-10), 9

happy are they that hear their detractions
~ *Much Ado About Nothing* (II.iii.229-230), 77

happy is your Grace
~ *As You Like It* (II.i.18-20), 129

harmony of their tongues
~ *The Tempest* (III.i.39-42), 13

heaping friendships
~ *The Winter's Tale* (IV.ii.18-20), 70

heart-blood of beauty
~ *Troilus and Cressida* (III.i.32-33), 28

heart-burned an hour after
~ *Much Ado About Nothing* (II.i.3-4), 52

heat and flame of thy distemper
~ *Hamlet* (III.iv.123-124), 151

heaven hath a hand
~ *Richard II* (V.ii.37-38), 140

heavenly rhetoric
~ *Love's Labor's Lost* (IV.iii.58), 30

heaven's breath smells wooingly
~ *Macbeth* (I.vi.5-6), 18

hell is empty
~ *The Tempest* (I.ii.214-215), 179

hell itself should gape
~ *Hamlet* (I.ii.244-245), 113

hence! home, you idle creatures
~ *Julius Caesar* (I.i.1), 65

hold off the earth awhile
~ *Hamlet* (V.i.249-250), 184

holiday-time of [her] beauty
~ *The Merry Wives of Windsor* (II.i.2), 29

honest plain words
~ *Love's Labor's Lost* (V.ii.753), 152

honest, as this world goes
~ *Hamlet* (II.ii.178-179), 45

honeying and making love
~ *Hamlet* (III.iv.93), 10

hope and expectation
~ *Henry IV, Part One* (III.ii.36), 37

hour to hour, we ripe and ripe
~ *As You Like It* (II.vii.26-28), 138

how bitter a thing it is
~ *As You Like It* (V.ii.43-45), 16

humble and familiar courtesy
~ *Richard II* (I.iv.25-26), 120

hurly-burly's done
~ *Macbeth* (I.i.3-4), 90

idle shallow things
~ *Twelfth Night* (III.iv.123-124), 119

ill blows the wind
~ *Henry VI, Part Three* (II.v.55), 147

imitate the action of the tiger
~ *Henry V* (III.i.3-6), 106

infinite deal of nothing
~ *The Merchant of Venice*
(I.i.114-118), 157

ingratitude! thou marble-hearted fiend
~ *King Lear* (I.iv.259), 114

innocent flower
~ *Macbeth* (I.v.66), 121

invincible unconquered spirit
~ *Henry VI, Part One* (IV.ii.31-32), 92

jests at scars
~ *Romeo and Juliet* (II.ii.1), 166

jocund day stands tiptoe
~ *Romeo and Juliet* (III.v.9-10), 97

kernel in this light nut
~ *All's Well That Ends Well* (II.v.43), 43

kindle, not to quench
~ *Coriolanus* (III.i.195-196), 143

kingdoms are clay
~ *Antony and Cleopatra* (I.i.35-37), 95

knit up in their distractions
~ *The Tempest* (III.iii.89-90), 69

lady far more beautiful
~ *The Taming of the Shrew,*
(Induction.ii.62-63), 27

lady tongue
~ *Much Ado About Nothing*
(II.i.274-275), 110

lards the lean earth
~ *Henry IV, Part One* (II.ii.109), 50

laurel victory
~ *Antony and Cleopatra* (I.iii.99-101), 88

lay on, Macduff
~ *Macbeth* (V.viii.33-34), 107

let slip the dogs of war
~ *Julius Caesar* (III.i.273), 108

life's fitful fever
~ *Macbeth* (III.ii.23), 133

light winning
~ *The Tempest* (I.ii.452-453), 147

lions make leopards tame
~ *Richard II* (I.i.174), 89

lips, two blushing pilgrims
~ *Romeo and Juliet* (I.v.95-96), 58

live in thy heart
~ *Much Ado About Nothing*
(V.ii.102-104), 61

look upon his like again
~ *Hamlet* (I.ii.187-188), 124

love is merely a madness
~ *As You Like It* (III.ii.400-402), 21

love of Love and her soft hours
~ *Antony and Cleopatra* (I.i.44-45), 49

love, be moderate
~ *The Merchant of Venice*
(III.ii.111-114), 11

love, in faith
~ *Troilus and Cressida* (III.i.127), 19

lovely April of her prime
~ *Sonnet 3* (10), 29

love's firm votary
~ *The Two Gentlemen of Verona*
(III.ii.58), 161

love's heavy burden
~ *Romeo and Juliet* (I.iv.22), 10

love's stories
~ *A Midsummer Night's Dream*
(II.ii.121-122), 31

loved not at first sight
~ *As You Like It* (III.v.82), 6

loved not wisely
~ *Othello* (V.ii.344), 15

lover may bestride the gossamers
~ *Romeo and Juliet* (II. vi.18-20), 162

lovers run into strange capers
~ *As You Like It* (II.iv.54-55), 21

loves to hear himself talk
~ *Romeo and Juliet* (II.iv.147-149), 48

lunatic, the lover, and the poet
~ *A Midsummer Night's Dream*
(V.i.7-8), 22

lusty stealth of nature
~ *King Lear* (I.ii.11), 13

lusty wench
~ *The Taming of the Shrew*
(II.i.160-162), 14

madam wife, sit by my side
~ *The Taming of the Shrew*
(Induction.ii.142-144), 57

madcap hath heaven lent us here
~ *King John* (I.i.84), 68

maid of grace
~ *Love's Labor's Lost* (I.i.137), 34

maids are May
~ *As You Like It* (IV.i.148-149), 60

makes him, and it mars him
~ *Macbeth* (II.iii.32), 144

man hath his desires
~ *As You Like It* (III.iii.83), 56

mars's hot minion
~ *The Tempest* (IV.i.98), 108

master a grief
~ *Much Ado About Nothing*
(III.ii.28-29), 152

masters of their fates
~ *Julius Caesar* (I.ii.139-141), 76

matter with less art
~ *Hamlet* (II.ii.95), 49

may-morn of his youth
~ *Henry V* (I.ii.120-121), 91

mend your speech
~ *King Lear* (I.i.94), 65

merrily, merrily shall I live
~ *The Tempest* (V.i.93-94), 94

merry, nimble, stirring spirit
~ *Love's Labor's Lost* (V.ii.16), 96

mickle is the powerful grace
~ *Romeo and Juliet* (II.iii.15-16), 97

milksop, one that never in his life
~ *Richard III* (V.iii.325-326), 51

mince it in love
~ *Henry V* (V.ii.126-127), 17

mirror of all courtesy
~ *Henry VIII* (II.i.53), 36

mirror up to nature
~ *Hamlet* (III.ii.22), 141

moderate lamentation is the right
~ *All's Well That Ends Well* (I.i.55-56), 130

modest doubt
~ *Troilus and Cressida* (II.ii.15-16), 177

money go before
~ *The Merry Wives of Windsor* (II.ii.168-169), 152

morn in russet mantle clad
~ *Hamlet* (I.i.166), 97

mortal paradise of such sweet flesh
~ *Romeo and Juliet* (III.ii.80-82), 40

music be the food of love
~ *Twelfth Night* (I.i.1), 17

music, moody food
~ *Antony and Cleopatra* (II.v.1-2), 17

music of his own vain tongue
~ *Love's Labor's Lost* (I.i.166-167), 47

naked to mine enemies
~ *Henry VIII* (III.ii.455-457), 78

natural graces that extinguish art
~ *Henry VI, Part One* (V.iii.191-192), 34

nature and fortune joined
~ *King John* (III.i.52), 117

nature might stand up and say
~ *Julius Caesar* (V.v.73-75), 123

nature there's no blemish
~ *Twelfth Night* (III.iv.367-368), 32

nature whom passion could not shake
~ *Othello* (IV.i.265-266), 18

needful bits and curbs
~ *Measure for Measure* (I.iii.20), 66

never, never, never, never, never
~ *King Lear* (V.iii.307-309), 126

nimbly and sweetly recommends itself
~ *Macbeth* (I.vi.1-3), 94

nimble-footed madcap
~ *Henry IV, Part One* (IV.i.95), 96

noble mind is here o'erthrown
~ *Hamlet* (III.i.150), 127

noble ruin of her magic
~ *Antony and Cleopatra* (III.x.18), 21

noble wife
~ *Julius Caesar* (II.i.303), 59

nothing can we call our own but death
~ *Richard II* (III.ii.152-154), 130

nothing in his life became him
~ *Macbeth* (I.iv.7-8), 124

o'erflow with joy
~ *All's Well That Ends Well* (II.iv.46-47), 96

old till thou hadst been wise
~ *King Lear* (I.v.44), 46

once more unto the breach
~ *Henry V* (III.i.1). 108

out, out, brief candle
~ *Macbeth* (V.v.23-28). 101

outsport discretion
~ *Othello* (II.iii.2-3), 143

outstrip all praise
~ *The Tempest* (IV.i.10-11), 59

owe more tears to this dead man
~ *Julius Caesar* (V.iii.101-102), 128

palpable hit
~ *Hamlet* (V.ii.281), 79

**paragons description and
wild fame**
~ *Othello* (II.i.61-62), 28

pardon after execution
~ *Henry VIII* (IV.ii.120-121), 78

passion's slave
~ *Hamlet* (III.ii.71-74), 71

past hope, past cure, past help
~ *Romeo and Juliet* (IV.i.45), 103

pattern of all patience
~ *King Lear* (III.ii.37), 74

peril in thine eye
~ *Romeo and Juliet* (II.ii.71-72), 8

pert and nimble spirit
~ *A Midsummer Night's Dream* (I.i.13), 96

physic the tavern affords
~ *Henry VI, Part One* (III.i.146), 181

pie is freed
~ *Henry VIII* (I.i.52-53), 76

pillar of the world
~ *Antony and Cleopatra* (I.i.11-13), 19

play my part in fortune's pageant
~ *Henry VI, Part Two* (I.ii.66-67), 112

**play with mammets and to tilt
with lips**
~ *Henry IV, Part One* (II.iii.91-93), 109

**pleased heaven to try me
with affliction**
~ *Othello* (IV.ii.48-53), 150

preserved when Fortune takes
~ *Othello* (I.iii.206-207), 149

pretty piece of flesh
~ *Romeo and Juliet* (I.i.29), 25

profits of the mind
~ *Measure for Measure* (I.iv.58-61), 172

project gather to a head
~ *The Tempest* (V.i.1), 121

promise of his age
~ *Much Ado About Nothing* (I.i.13-14), 82

**proportion both of thanks
and payment**
~ *Macbeth* (I.iv.18-21), 165

**purpose more grave
and wrinkled**
~ *Measure for Measure* (I.iii.4-6), 183

rack of this tough world
~ *King Lear* (V.iii.314-316), 127

**radiant, exquisite, and
unmatchable beauty**
~ *Twelfth Night* (I.v.170-171), 27

**rail against our mistress
the world**
~ *As You Like It* (III.ii.277-279), 103

rash and most unfortunate man
~ *Othello* (V.ii.283), 64

reason sits in the wind
~ *Antony and Cleopatra* (III.x.35-36), 174

rejoice beyond a common joy
~ *The Tempest* (V.i.206-208), 168

replete with choice of all delights
~ *Henry VI, Part One* (V.v.16-17), 26

reproof of chance
~ *Troilus and Cressida* (I.iii.33-34), 145

reputation, reputation, reputation
~ *Othello* (II.iii.262-264), 118

resolution and the briefest end
~ *Antony and Cleopatra* (IV.xv.90-91), 102

ripeness is all
~ *King Lear* (V.ii.9-11), 137

rise by sin
~ *Measure for Measure* (II.i.38), 149

robbed that smiles
~ *Othello* (I.iii.208), 83

rogue and peasant slave
~ *Hamlet* (II.ii.550), 115

run to your houses
~ *Julius Caesar* (I.i.53-55), 114

sated with his body
~ *Othello* (I.iii.350-351), 20

savage bull doth bear the yoke
~ *Much Ado About Nothing* (I.i.261), 62

scape not the thunderbolt
~ *Antony and Cleopatra* (II.v.77), 149

scars to move laughter only
~ *Coriolanus* (III.iii.52), 106

scorched the snake, not killed it
~ *Macbeth* (III.ii.13-15), 176

screw your courage to the sticking place
~ *Macbeth* (I.vii.59-61), 107

searching of thy wound
~ *As You Like It* (II.iv.44-45), 179

self-love
~ *Henry V* (II.iv.74), 178

sell when you can
~ *As You Like It* (III.v.60), 175

serpent heart
~ *Romeo and Juliet* (III.ii.73-74), 41

set my life upon a cast
~ *Richard III* (V.iv.9-10), 104

set you up a glass
~ *Hamlet* (III.iv.18-20), 141

shake the yoke of inauspicious stars
~ *Romeo and Juliet* (V.iii.109-112), 126

shaken as we are
~ *Henry IV, Part One* (I.i.1), 79

shallow fools
~ *Much Ado About Nothing* (V.i.232-234), 180

shameful conquest of itself
~ *Richard II* (II.i.65-66), 90

sharp-toothed unkindness
~ *King Lear* (II.iv.134-135), 112

sharper than a serpent's tooth
~ *King Lear* (I.iv.288-289), 171

show more mirth
~ *As You Like It* (I.ii.3-4), 172

shut up in measureless content
~ *Macbeth* (II.i.16-17), 95

sick that surfeit with too much
~ *The Merchant of Venice* (I.ii.5-7), 142

sigh no more, ladies
~ *Much Ado About Nothing* (II.iii.62-65), 160

sighed upon a midnight pillow
~ *As You Like It* (II.iv.26-27), 7

silver livery of advised age
~ *Henry VI, Part Two* (V.ii.46-47), 167

sin for a man to labor
~ *Henry IV, Part One* (I.ii.104-105), 176

skirmish of wit between them
~ *Much Ado About Nothing*
(I.i.63-64), 111

slander music
~ *Much Ado About Nothing*
(II.iii.44-45), 51

slander's venomed spear
~ *Richard II* (I.i.171), 118

slanderous tongue
~ *Measure for Measure* (III.ii.187-188), 119

slave had forty thousand lives
~ *Othello* (III.iii.442-443), 105

slenderly known himself
~ *King Lear* (I.i.293), 44

solemnize this day
~ *King John* (III.i.77-80), 98

sorrow leave a while to tutor me
~ *Richard II* (IV.i.166-167), 126

sorrows to be proud
~ *King John* (III.i.68), 132

soul brought forth her prodigy
~ *Richard II* (II.ii.64), 47

soul hath elbow room
~ *King John* (V.vii.28), 95

soul hath her content so absolute
~ *Othello* (II.i.189-193), 57

soul in bliss
~ *King Lear* (IV.vii.45-47), 135

soul of this man is his clothes
~ *All's Well That Ends Well*
(II.v.43-45), 43

soul rememb'ring my
good friends
~ *Richard II* (II.iii.46-47), 69

soul's food
~ *The Two Gentlemen of Verona*
(II.vii.15), 6

soul's joy
~ *Othello* (II.i.184-186), 163

speaks poniards
~ *Much Ado About Nothing*
(II.i.247-250), 170

special providence in the fall
~ *Hamlet* (V.ii.219-220), 138

spend word for word with me
~ *The Two Gentlemen of Verona*
(II.iv.41-42), 110

spendthrift is he of his tongue
~ *The Tempest* (II.i.24), 48

spirit chased than enjoyed
~ *The Merchant of Venice*
(II.vi.12-13), 59

spirit of persuasion
~ *Henry IV, Part One* (I.ii.152-153), 77

sport and revels
~ *Othello* (II.ii.5-6), 96

spotless reputation
~ *Richard II* (I.i.177-179), 117

stage of fools
~ *King Lear* (IV.vi.182-183), 136

stage, where every man must
play his part
~ *The Merchant of Venice* (I.i.77-79), 116

steals my purse steals trash
~ *Othello* (III.iii.157-161), 118

steal immortal blessing from her lips
~ *Romeo and Juliet* (III.iii.37), 10

stomachs, and we all but food
~ *Othello* (III.iv.104), 42

strawberry grows underneath the nettle
~ *Henry V* (I.i.60), 147

striving to better
~ *King Lear* (I.iv.346), 148

study what you most affect
~ *The Taming of the Shrew* (I.i.39-40), 182

sugared words
~ *Richard III* (III.i.13-14), 81

suggestion as a cat laps milk
~ *The Tempest* (II.i.288), 121

sun begins to gild
~ *The Two Gentlemen of Verona* (V.i.1), 98

superfluous and lust-dieted man
~ *King Lear* (IV.i.67), 43

sweet are the uses of adversity
~ *As You Like It* (II.i.12), 185

sweet creature of bombast
~ *Henry IV, Part One* (II.iv.326-327), 47

sweet hope's aim
~ *The Comedy of Errors* (III.ii.63), 6

sweet life's loss
~ *King John* (IV.iii.106), 128

take note, take note, O world
~ *Othello* (III.iii.377-378), 115

taste sack and drink it
~ *Henry IV, Part One* (II.iv.455-459), 53

taste the wages of their virtue
~ *King Lear* (V.iii.303-305), 87

tempted... another thing to fall
~ *Measure for Measure* (II.i.17-18), 159

tenders of his affection to me
~ *Hamlet* (I.iii.99-100), 12

theme of honor's tongue
~ *Henry IV, Part One* (I.i.81), 37

theme of honor and renown
~ *Troilus and Cressida* (II.ii.199-200), 36

things by season seasoned are
~ *The Merchant of Venice* (V.i.107-108), 155

things in heaven and earth
~ *Hamlet* (I.v.166-167), 174

things past redress
~ *Richard II* (II.iii.171), 143

things sweet to taste
~ *Richard II* (I.iii.236), 148

thorny point of bare distress
~ *As You Like It* (II.vii.94-96), 136

thoughts are ripe in mischief
~ *Twelfth Night* (V.i.129), 104

tide in the affairs of men
~ *Julius Caesar* (IV.iii.218-223), 111

tiger's heart
~ *Henry VI, Part Three* (I.iv.137), 169

time and the hour runs through
~ *Macbeth* (I.iii.146-147), 150

time's ruin, beauty's wrack
~ *The Rape of Lucrece* (1451), 39

to thine own self be true
~ *Hamlet* (I.iii.78-80), 173

toil of grace
~ *Antony and Cleopatra* (V.ii.348), 33

tomorrow, and tomorrow, and tomorrow
~ *Macbeth* (V.v.19-21), 100

toothache patiently
~ *Much Ado About Nothing* (V.i.35-36), 151

touch, a touch, I do confess
~ *Hamlet* (V.ii.286), 79

trappings and the suits of woe
~ *Hamlet* (I.ii.85-86), 125

trifles light as air
~ *Othello* (III.iii.322-24), 15

true beauty till this night
~ *Romeo and Juliet* (I.v.52-53), 5

turn, hell-hound, turn
~ *Macbeth* (V.viii.3), 167

unclasp'd to thee the book
~ *Twelfth Night* (I.iv.13-14), 70

undone, and forfeited to cares
~ *All's Well That Ends Well* (II.iii.267), 63

uneasy lies the head
~ *Henry IV, Part Two* (III.i.31), 80

unhoused free condition
~ *Othello* (I.ii.25-28), 61

unstooping firmness
~ *Richard II* (I.i.121), 120

unyoked humor of your idleness
~ *Henry IV, Part One* (I.ii.195-196), 67

victory sits on our helms
~ *Richard III* (V.iii.351), 90

villainy you teach me
~ *The Merchant of Venice* (III.i.71-73), 105

violent delights have violent ends
~ *Romeo and Juliet* (II.vi.9-11), 22

votary to fond desire
~ *The Two Gentlemen of Verona* (I.i.52), 9

watered his new plants
~ *Coriolanus* (V.vi.23), 45

we are amazed
~ *Richard II* (III.iii.72-73), 116

weary, stale, flat and unprofitable
~ *Hamlet* (I.ii.133-134), 99

weed who art so lovely fair
~ *Othello* (IV.ii.67-69), 40

well cudgeled
~ *Othello* (II.iii.365-366), 79

well-practiced wise directions
~ *Henry IV, Part Two* (V.ii.120-121), 84

what cannot be eschewed
~ *The Merry Wives of Windsor* (V.v.237), 145

what wound did ever heal
~ *Othello* (II.iii.370-371), 150

what's done cannot be undone
~ *Macbeth* (V.i.68), 144

what's gone and what's past help
~ *The Winter's Tale* (III.ii.222-223), 130

wheel is come full circle
~ *King Lear* (V.iii.175), 78

whip hypocrisy
~ *Love's Labor's Lost* (IV.iii.149), 106

whirligig of time
~ *Twelfth Night* (V.i.376-377), 77

white hairs
~ *Henry IV, Part Two* (V.v.48), 46

wide and universal theatre
~ *As You Like It* (II.vii.137-139), 130

widows howl, new orphans cry
~ *Macbeth* (IV.iii.4-6), 136

wilt not utter what thou dost not know
~ *Henry IV, Part One* (II.iii.110-112), 44

win a paradise
~ *Love's Labor's Lost* (IV.iii.70-71), 55

wind sits in the shoulder
~ *Hamlet* (I.iii.56), 165

wine of life is drawn
~ *Macbeth* (II.iii.94-96), 127

wise and love
~ *Troilus and Cressida* (III.ii.156-157), 63

wise, fair, and true
~ *The Merchant of Venice* (II.vi.56-57), 59

wisely and slow
~ *Romeo and Juliet* (II.iii.94), 73

withered and so wild
~ *Macbeth* (I.iii.39-42), 53

woman's heart grossly grew captive
~ *Richard III* (IV.i.78-79), 9

women's eyes this doctrine
~ *Love's Labor's Lost* (IV.iii.347-350), 29

woo peaceably
~ *Much Ado About Nothing* (V.ii.72), 23

woo'd in haste
~ *The Taming of the Shrew* (III.ii.11), 63

world must be peopled
~ *Much Ado About Nothing* (II.iii.242), 56

world of vile ill-favored faults
~ *The Merry Wives of Windsor* (III.iv.32-33), 153

world's large spaces
~ *Troilus and Cressida* (II.ii.161-162), 28

world's large tongue
~ *Love's Labor's Lost* (V.ii.842-843), 49

worm in the bud
~ *Twelfth Night* (II.iv.110-112), 163

wounds invisible that love's keen arrows make
~ *As You Like It* (III.v.30-31), 19

wring your heart
~ *Hamlet* (III.iv.34-35), 141

years but young
~ *The Two Gentlemen of Verona* (II.iv.69-70), 39

young man married
~ *All's Well That Ends Well* (II.iii.298), 62

young men's love
~ *Romeo and Juliet* (II.iii.67-68), 14

youth's a stuff
~ *Twelfth Night* (II.iii.47-52), 16

Printed in Great Britain
by Amazon

79547001R00129